A Chapter of Santal folklore

A Chapter of Santal folklore

By
P.O. BODDING

GYAN

Published by

Gyan Publishing House
5, Ansari Road
Daryaganj, New Delhi-110002
Phone: 011-47034999, 9811692060
E-mail: books@gyanbooks.com

Distribution Network
gyanbooks.com
India, USA, Canada, UK, Australia, France

ISBN : 978-81-212-6759-5 (PB)
First Published, 1924

2nd Impression 2022

Printed at: Gyan Press, Delhi.

A Chapter of Santal folklore
Author: P.O. BODDING

ROYAL FREDERIK UNIVERSITY

PUBLICATIONS

OF THE INDIAN INSTITUTE

I, 2. A CHAPTER OF SANTAL FOLKLORE

BY P. O. BODDING

1924

A CHAPTER OF SANTAL FOLKLORE

BY

P. O. BODDING

A discussion of the different questions of folkloristic and ethnological nature which would naturally present themselves in connection with the tales and stories here edited and translated will find its proper place when my collections have been published in their entirety. Here, therefore, only a few introductory remarks.

The present writer received, whilst still a child, his first introduction to folk-tales through an old nurse; the interest thus awakened has followed him ever since, and he took it with him out to India now nearly thirty-four years ago. I had not been among the Santals many months, before I heard of and also commenced to collect folk-tales of theirs. The first one to tell me any such was a young man who had heard some tales from his mother and grandmother. When I came to Mohulpahari, my present home in India, I got some more tales from an elderly Santal *guru*, named PHAGU from the village of Dhaka, near Mohulpahari, the same man who has furnished the songs printed in the book 'The Traditions and Institutions of the Santals' (in Santali, taken down by the late Mr. SKREFSRUD from the dictation of Kolean *guru*, 2nd edition, Benagaria, 1916, edited by the present writer), and who also dictated to me a much more circumstantial version of the traditions than that found in the book mentioned.

It did not, however, take long before I understood that it would require more time than I had at my disposal to take down the stories, the more so as I soon found out that here were materials for a large collection, and I naturally wanted to collect as much as possible. There was another consideration which weighed much with me: I tried to be accurate, but there was always the possibility that the tales might be more or less tainted by passing through a European brain, both as to language and as to contents. It would be very much preferable to get the tales written down by a Santal.

It so happened about a year after my arrival at Mohulpahari that I had a man, SAGRAM MURMU by name, sent to me to be a helper in my work in connection with the Santali language. I soon discovered that this man had a natural ability of writing his own language. He was consequently asked to write down all stories he knew, and whenever I heard of a fresh story, the person in question was asked to tell it to him, and he wrote it down.

It was a private arrangement between us. He used his leisure hours to write, and was paid per page by me. It led to his hunting up people of whom he heard that they might have stories to tell. His writing had also another result. When people heard that there was a market for such, some persons who could do so wrote down stories they knew and brought them. One who did this was the young man first mentioned above, who in the meantime had been appointed postmaster at Mohulpahari. Another one was his wife.

In the course of time the collection has grown to quite a small library. How many folk-tales there may be in my collection, I have not counted. It is large.

The majority of the tales have been written by the above mentioned Sagram Murmu, who hails from a village in the Godda Subdivision of the Santal Parganas district, Bihar. When no remark is made, it is to be understood that he is the writer. Tales put on paper by others have a note to show who has written them.

Sagram Murmu came to Mohulpahari in the early part of 1892, and has remained there ever since, his special work having been to be one of my 'living dictionaries'. He has passed what in our parts of India is called the Lower Primary examination in Hindi — it amounts to very little. What he else knows, he has picked up himself. This is just mentioned to show that he has not been long enough in school to get his language 'educated'. He is a Santal from the village, the genuine article, well acquainted with the customs, ideas, and superstitions of his own people, now old, well up in the sixties, looking just the picture of a folk-tale teller. He has a tendency towards 'preaching' and moralizing, and may be somewhat headstrong. This does not, however, affect his tales, except that he now and then furnishes them with a 'tail' giving vent to his own opinions.

The tales are, as will be understood, written in genuine Santali, without any attempt at polishing, only obvious errors or slips of the pen having been corrected. Before the missionaries came, the Santals had no written language. What they had of 'literature' was all stowed away in their memory. Incantations, songs and certain other matters are in a stereotype form, often such as not to be always properly understood by the present generation. This is not the case with the folk-tales, where, within certain limits, there is full freedom for the narrator. The language of these may consequently vary as to individual form and expression. There is no literary style. Santali has not like some other Indian languages, as e. g. Bengali, a high or literary form, a colloquial and a vulgar form. The language of these tales is just as the people speak.

The translation is literal, as far as compatible with good sense, one reason for such literality being that the idiom of a language often throws light on the mentality of the people. The object of editing these tales and stories is not to tell interesting tales, but to give those who study folklore genuine and reliable material.

The translation has been supplied with a number of explanatory notes, where it seemed necessary or desirable. In several cases the Santali word or a commonly used word from another Indian language has been used, to avoid long explanations or paraphrases. Such have been explained in the notes. A number of notes giving ethnological information has also been added, in the hope that they will help the reader to appreciate certain details.

The Santali text will furnish excellent material for the study of the Santali language, which is of considerable interest in several respects.

— There are a few things more to be mentioned.

These tales are the property of the Santals. Many of them are undoubtedly autochthonous, some may be the common property of the Santals and other neighbouring races, and it may at the present time be impossible to decide whose property they originally were. A number may have been acquired from other peoples who live among the Santals, often in the same villages, from people whom they daily meet.

I do not at the moment remember any stories borrowed from Mohammedan sources; if there are such, they are very few. The Santals seem to look upon the Mohammedans as people quite different from themselves, and with distrust. The above mentioned Kolean *guru* says in one place in the printed traditions: "More than all other races we resent and abhor the *turuk*." Now *turuk* in Santali really means the Mussulman cavalry, of which the Santals had experience in former days. Here the word is used in such a way that it seems to include people of that persuasion also.

Those from whom they have adopted stories are Hindus of all sorts, generally low caste. With these they have much in common. From literary sources I do not think any Santal tales have been borrowed, the only exceptions being Æsop's fables, acquired through schoolbooks, and not by any means common property. I might just mention that I have, among the tales, a Santali version of the Ramayana, very likely the result of Santals seeing a puppet show, and listening to the stories told by the showman.

It is generally not difficult to tell at once whether it is an originally borrowed tale or not. However this may be, the stories are all in Santali garb, and adapted to Santal customs and Santal ideas, just as when a foreign word is adopted by the language: it has to be adapted to and made conform with the demands of the phonetic laws of the language.

It should be noted that the tales always move in a Santal world, and are exponents of the Santal mode of living, speaking and thinking. Many of the tales are good pictures of life, such as is met with in the Santal villages and homes. In this way they furnish true material for learning to know the people.

To the Santals the stories represent several things. They may be intended to amuse, to explain, e. g. natural phenomena or strange matters, to teach, to point a moral, to give an explanation or perhaps an excuse for doing or omitting to do something, &c.

According to their contents, they are told or recited on different occasions. An old mother, a grandmother, an aunt or other elderly person may tell stories they know to the children, just like we ourselves in our childhood heard stories from our old nurses.

I have, however, an impression that most of these stories are more the property of men than of women.

When Santals sit together without having anything special to do, somebody may start telling a story, or somebody may ask for such a one. Some one of the party may ask about something. This reminds another of an incident of a story, which is mentioned, and a third asks whether they have not heard this. After some talking, one man will commence to tell. I have happened to be present on such occasions. Likely most of them, if not all, have heard the tale, or know it. As the narrator proceeds, he is again and again interrupted by acclamations of approval, grunts of satisfaction and enjoyment, and the like. Then the narrator may not be quite sure as to some details, and somebody offers the correct rendering, or there may come corrections from one or more of the party, who believe themselves to know certain particulars better. They are all of them in it. It is very amusing to be present and listen.

If a Santal is asked when these tales are told, he will nearly always say it is when they watch on the threshing floor. When the rains are over and the Santals commence reaping their paddy, the sheaves are carried to the threshing floor, a small bit of levelled ground, beaten hard and plastered with cow-dung, on a higher level than the rice fields, but generally not far away from them, to obviate too much trouble in carrying the sheaves. During the harvest time people often live more on the threshing floor than in their homes. In a corner a booth is always erected, a few slender poles put up against each other, the whole covered with straw, having a tiny opening at the floor. Here people live for days and weeks. Thieves lurk about at this time, and it is necessary to watch the stacks of sheaves on the threshing floor, and also so far as possible the adjoining unreaped paddy-fields. Generally several families have their threshing floors in one place, close to each other. So they watch together, and to keep awake and pass the long hours of night, they have to resort to different devices; one of these is to tell folk-tales. They enjoy them, and see them enacted, so to say, before their mental vision.

Folk-tales belong to a special period of cultural development; they presuppose and demand a certain state of mentality, when the critical powers are not as yet sufficiently developed to prevent certain flights of imagination or the enjoyment of obvious impossibilities. Like so many other peoples, the Santals are passing from the stage where folk-tales can exist. I may not be right, but I am under the impression that many of the folk-tales collected by myself are getting out of use and being lost. I do not think it would be possible at the present day to trace all those that have been secured for my collection. The vast majority of them was collected during my first twenty years in India. By that time, the Santal supply had been more or less drained. Still it happens, even now, that a new story is heard; but it is very seldom.

p. t. Lõken, Heradsbygd, Norway, 17th July 1923.

P. O. Bodding.

As to the pronunciation of the letters used in writing Santali, the following may be noted: The system followed is very much the same as that recommended by the ROYAL ASIATIC SOCIETY for transliteration of Indian languages, with a few exceptions and some additions, made necessary by Santali having some sounds peculiar to itself.

The vowels, when without diacritical marks, are pronounced very much as in Norwegian: a (mbw) like *a* in *father,* — e (mfn or mfw) like *e* in Norw. *se* or Engl. *men,* — i (hfn or hfw) like *i* in Norw. *mine* or Engl. *bit,* — o (mbnr or mbwr) like *o* in Norw. *stor* or *sort,* — u (hbnr or hbwr or hmnr) like *ou* in French *tour,* or *u* in Engl. *put* and Norw. *hus.*

Vowels with a dash below are the open vowel sounds, as against the unmarked close sound: e̱ (lfn or lfw) like the sound in Engl. *air, fat,* — o̱ (lbnr or lbwr or lmn) like the sound in Engl. *law, not,* or Norw. *monne.* In suffixes, postpositions and personal pronouns, the open e̱ and o̱ sounds are not marked.

Vowels with a dot below are peculiar Santali sounds, tentatively called resultant. Only two are used here, ạ and ọ: ạ is, to an untrained ear, something between Engl. *but* and *hat,* — ọ is a modified mbnr sound.

All vowels may be long or short.

All vowels may be nasalized; this is shown by the circumflex ˜ above the vowel; cf. the French pronunciation of e. g. *dans, ancien, bon.*

With reference to the consonants, it should be noted that all stops are either unaspirated or fully aspirated (this shown by *h,* written after the stop consonant).

With this reservation, the velars are pronounced as in English.

g is always like *g* in Engl. *garb, get,* not like *g* in *gentle,* — ṅ is the velar nasal, like *ng* in Engl. *song,* — k' is the checked consonant *k* without its offglide.

The palatals may be compared to the corresponding Italian sounds.

c and j are palatals, not compound sounds, in so far differing from Engl. *ch* and soft *g.*

ń is the palatal nasal, pronounced something like Spanish *ñ.*

y is never a vowel as in Scandinavian languages, but always the open medio-palatal fricative sound, something like *j* in e. g. Danish *ja,* or *veje.*

c' is the checked consonant *c* without its offglide.

The cacuminals are all pronounced with inverted tongue-tip; they are written like the corresponding dentals, with a dot below:

ṭ is like *rt* in Norw. dial. *bort,* — ḍ is like *rd* in Norw. dial. *gjorde,* — ṇ is like *rdn* in Norw. dial. *tordne,* — ṛ is like the socalled thick *l* in Norw. dial. *sol, ola, jord.*

The dentals are pure dentals, not supradentals; pronounced very much like the corresponding letters in Italian.

t' is the checked consonant *t* without its offglide.

The stopped labials are pronounced very much like the corresponding Engl. sounds, excepting that, as remarked above, the unaspirated letters are unaspirated.

The open labials are like the corresponding English sounds *v* and *w.*

p' is the checked consonant *p* without its offglide.

The sibilant is always pure dental voiceless, like *s* in Engl. *sink.*

The checked consonants, of which Santali has four, are written as the corresponding full consonant with an apostrophe.

For a full description of the Santali sounds and pronunciation the reader is referred to the writer's book 'Materials for a Santali Grammar I. Mostly phonetic.' Dumka 1922.

BOṄGA TULUÇ BAPLA AKAN HO̱Ṛ REAṄ KẠHNIKO

1. Kaḍa gupi koṛa reaṅ

Sedae jo̱khe̱n, kathae, miťťaṅ koṛa kaḍae gupi kan tahẽ̱kana, ado̱ din hiloḱge ạḍi ńindạ anẹć kaḍae aderkoa.

Ado̱ kathae, miť din do̱ ạyuṕ siṅgạṛ jo̱khe̱ć oṛaḱte kaḍae laga ạguyeťko tahẽ̱kana. Ado̱ e̱n hiloḱge miť ho̱ṛko husiťkedea; uni do̱ kuṛi boṅgae tahẽ̱kana. Ado̱ uni boṅga do̱ko idikedete do̱bạṭiạre hesaḱ dare tahẽ̱kana; o̱ṇḍe̱ge kiriạkedete binidạko emadete ona hesaḱ dareregeko khil jalaťkadea. Ado̱ e̱n hiloḱ ạyuṕ siṅgạṛge uni koṛa do̱, kathae, ona do̱bạṭiạ hesaḱ dare se̱ntegeye ạguyeťko tahẽ̱kana. Ado̱ uni kuṛi do̱ ona hesaḱ dare jalaťregeye teṅgo akane ńe̱lkedea. Khange uni koṛa do̱e bujhạukeťa, nui kuṛi do̱ oka khon co̱e ať hẹćakan, ar baṅkhane usạťakana; onka mo̱nreye hudiskeťa. Ado̱ se̱n sorkate bae kulikedea, Henda peṛa, okaren kanam?

Ado̱ uni kuṛiye me̱nkeťa, Ạḍi sạṅgiṅren kanaṅ, peṛa.

Ado̱ uni koṛae me̱nkeťa ać mo̱nre, Jāhāren kangeye, eṅgateṅ baḍha idikaea; noa dare buṭạre do̱ cedaḱe tahe̱na? Ale oṛaḱteṅ idikaea, e̱ṇḍe̱ tahẽ̱ aṅgakate ado̱e jāhā se̱noḱge. Onka mo̱nre bujhạu baṛakate uni kuṛiye metadea, Henda peṛa, ať hẹćakana se̱m ceťa? Ar baṅkhan dela iṅiṅ baḍha idikama.

Ado̱ uni kuṛiye me̱nkeťa, Hẽ̱, peṛa, e̱ntem baḍha idiń khan do̱ń se̱nkoḱa.

Henda peṛa, e̱ntem oka atoren kana? Ma ṭhikte lạiaṅme; inạ do̱ko kuliń khan, iń hõ̱ inageń lạia, ar baṅkhan ạuri do̱ okareniń lạia?

---

1 *Boṅga* is the Santali name for a spirit or a godling, considered evil or anyhow dangerous by the Santals. Besides the bongas regularly worshipped, a large number is supposed to live in the hills, in rivers, trees, pits, &c., both male and female. The Santals believe that bongas, more frequently female ones, may be married to or have sexual intercourse with human beings.

2 The pipol tree is *Ficus religiosa*, L. The common Bengali or Hindi name is used here. Even among the Santals it is considered as something special, it being held to be of use also in the world to come. This is likely due to foreign influence; they do not otherwise consider the tree sacred. The witches are reported to travel through the air on these trees, just as their European sisters ride on broomsticks.

3 It is very common with young girls to sulk, 'furte' as it is called in Norwegian. It is an ordinary thing with young wives, who run away from their husbands.

4 Friend is a term used by Santals when addressing strangers, specially when meeting such on the way and deeming them Santals.

STORIES OF SANTALS MARRIED TO PEOPLE OF THE NETHERWORLD

1. THE YOUNG MAN AND THE BONGA[1] GIRL

ONCE upon a time long ago, it is told, a young man was occupied herding buffaloes. It was his habit to bring the buffaloes home only when it was late night.

So it came to pass that he one day at nightfall was driving the buffaloes home. Now that same day the people had exorcized a certain man there, and the spirit they had expelled was a female bonga. They had taken this bonga to a junction of two ways where a pipol[2] tree was standing; here they had adjured her, given her a gift of dismissal, and then fastened her to that pipol tree. As told, it happened at nightfall that very day that this young man was driving his cattle towards this pipol tree standing at the crossway. He caught sight of the girl standing up against the pipol tree. The young man said to himself: this girl has lost her way and has come here from somewhere, or otherwise she is in the dumps[3]. So he reasoned in his mind. What was then more natural for him than to go up to her and ask her: "Well, friend[4], wherefrom are you?"

The girl answered: "I am from very far away, friend."

The young man then said to himself: "She may be from anywhere; dash it[5], I shall take her along. Why should she remain here under this tree? I shall take her to our house, then she may stay there until dawn and so go wherever she likes." So he was thinking in his mind and spoke to the girl: "Look here, friend, have you lost yourself coming here, or how? Otherwise come along, I shall take you with me."

"Yes, friend," the girl said, "if you take me along I shall go."

"Look here, friend, from which village are you then? Tell me that correctly. When they ask me about this, I shall tell them what you say. Else how should I tell wherefrom you are, at random?"

---

[5] The Santals do not swear in our sense of the word. They have, however, a number of expletives, more or less extensively used. They are not considered high language, and many object to their use. Others are so inured to them that they, if they do not have them, feel their language 'tailless', as they express themselves. All these expletives generally refer to the human anatomy. The word here employed has been so often used so as to have lost all meaning. I have not heard a Santal being able to explain what it really is. Originally it may have meant something like 'by the female principle', 'by the mother'.

Adọ kathae, mitṭań atoe lạiket́a, bańmań phalna atoren kana. Adọ uni kọṛae mẹnket́a. Acha bogege; adọ jāhā leka ńańamko hẹćlen khan dọle lạiakoa, ale ṭhen menaea mẹnte. Ẹnḍẹkhan cedaḱ nọnḍẹ dọm tahẹna? Dela ale oṛaḱtegeń idikama; aṅgalen khan adọ jāhā sẹngem calaḱ, ọntẹge calaḱme.

Adọ uni kuṛiye mẹnket́a, Hẹ̃, ẹntem idiń khan dọń calaḱa, ar bańkhan nẹnḍẹgeń tahẹ̃ aṅgaḱa.

Adọ uni kọṛae mẹnket́a, Dela ẹnte, khusitem calaḱ khan dọń idimea, ar jọrmọṭkate dọ ọhọń idilema.

Adọ uni kuṛiye mẹnket́a, Acha, khusitegeń calaḱa; menkhan iń metam kana, noa ti jaṅgare jạnumteń rampha akana, ona chaḍaokańme.

Adọe chaḍaokadea. Adọ kathae, tin hạbić unkinkin galmarao kan tahẹ̃kan, un hạbić kạḍa dọko teṅgo thir akan tahẹ̃kangea. Adọ uniye chaḍaokede khan, adọ kaḍakin lagakeťkoa. Adọ laga idiketko khan divheko jẹrẹť oḍokket́a kaḍa tọlko lạgiť. Adọ unreko kulikedea, Henda ya, nui dọ ọkọeyem ạgukedea? Ar uni kuṛi dọ racaregeye teṅgoakana, ar uni kọṛa dọ goṛateye bọlọyente kaḍae tọlketkoa. Adọ oḍokkate arhọ̃ko kuliyede kana, Henda ya, ọkọeyem ạgukedea, bạhu sẹ ọkọe?

Adọe metaťkoa, Mitṭań peṛa hoṛ kanae, hante khon iń baḍha ạguakadea.

Adọko bujhạuket́a, nui dọ bạhugeye ạgu akadea. Adọ piṇḍạre mạciko belket́teko họhọadea, Dela mạ̃i, nọnḍẹ piṇḍạte hijuḱme. Adọ piṇḍạteye rakaṕente mạcireye duṛuṕena. Adọ uni kuṛiko kuliyede kana, Henda mạ̃i, am dọm okaren kana?

Adọ uni kuṛiye mẹnket́a, Hana phalna atoren kanań.

Adọ okatem calaḱa?

Adọ uni kuṛiye mẹnket́a, Iń dọ usạť iń hẹćakana, jāhātege mẹ̃ť lutur ọnteń calaḱa; adọ kạḍa ạguko jọkhẹn hoṛreye ńamkidińteye metadińa, Dela ale oṛaḱteń idimea.

Adọ arhọ̃ uni kọṛako kulikedea, Henda ya, ma lạime, bạhu kanae sẹ bań?

Adọ uni kọṛae mẹnket́a, Bạhu dọe bań kana; adọ nitoḱ kạḍa ạguko jọkhẹn ona dọbạṭiạ hesaḱ dare ṭhene japaḱ akan tahẹ̃kana. Adọń ńẹlkede khan iń kulikedea, Henda peṛam okaren kana? Aṭakana sẹm usạť hoṛ kana? Cedaḱ am eskar nọnḍẹm tahẹna? Hoṛ họpọn kangeam? Delań idi toramea; ale oṛaḱre gitić aṅgaḱme, adọ setaḱlen khan, jāhā sẹngem calaḱ. Onka mẹnkateń ạgu dara akadea.

Adọ ẹnẹko thir baṛayena; kedoḱ dakako isińket́teko jọm baṛaket́a, uni kuṛi họ̃ko emadegea. Adọ parkomkoko ader baṛaket́a, ar uni kuṛi dọ pạṭiạko beladea; adọ ẹnẹko gitić aṅgayena.

---

6 Branches of trees with strong thorns are commonly used for fencing or blocking the way. A bonga may, it seems, acc. to their ideas, be shut up with the help of thorns. The thorn-trees most commonly found and used are the *Zizyphus Jujuba*, LAM., and the *Zizyphus oxyphylla*, EDGEW.

The exorcizing here above referred to is a very complicated and expensive affair. The bonga is not supposed to be seen, but to have taken possession of a man, who acts on behalf of the bonga. It is ordinarily only the *kisạ̃ṛ* bonga, a hobgoblin, very much resembling the Norwegian 'nisse', which is exorcized. What is here thought of, is not quite clear. It seems as if the bonga is supposed to have taken visible shape.

7 A mat is often used in lieu of a bedstead. To lie on a mat spread on the ground may imply sexual abstinence.

So she named a village, saying: "I am from such and such a village." The young man then said: "Well, that is all right; if now by any chance people should come searching for you, we shall tell them she is here. Why should you remain here? Come, I shall take you along to our house. Then to-morrow morning, if you want to go anywhere, go there."

"Yes," the girl answered, "if you take me along, I shall go, otherwise I shall remain here until dawn."

"Well then," the young man said, "if you come of your own free will, I shall take you with me. Against your will I should never take you away."

The girl then said: "Well, I shall come with pleasure; but I tell you my hands and feet are blocked up with thorns[6]; release me from those."

So he set her free. Now all the time they were talking together the buffaloes had been standing quiet. When he had set her free, they drove the buffaloes along; when they reached the house, the people lighted a lamp and brought that out to see to tie up the buffaloes. Then they asked him: "Look here, boy, who is this whom you have brought with you?" The girl was standing in the courtyard, whilst the young man went into the cattle-shed and tied the buffaloes up. When he came out again, they asked him once more: "Look here, laddie, whom have you brought? Is it a wife or what is it?"

"It is a friend," he answered, "I have brought her along from over there where I found her."

They consequently thought that he had brought the girl to be his wife. Thereupon they placed a stool on the veranda and called out to her: "Please, my girl, come here to the veranda." She then went up to the veranda and sat down on the stool, whereupon they commenced to question her: "Look here, my girl, which place do you belong to?"

"I am from such and such a distant village," the girl answered.

"And where are you going to?"

The girl then said: "I am in the dumps and have come to go in whatever direction my eyes and ears will take me. So when he was taking the buffaloes along, he found me on the way and said to me: Come along, I shall take you to our house."

Hereupon they once more asked the young man: "Look here, you boy, tell whether she is your wife or not."

"No," the young man answered, "she is not my wife. When I was driving the buffaloes along, she was leaning up against the pipol tree at the crossway. When I saw her, I asked her: Well, friend, wherefrom are you? Have you lost your way or are you in the dumps? Why do you remain here alone by yourself? Are you a Santal? Come, I shall take you with me; stay in our house for the night, then, as soon as it is morning, you may go wherever you like. Having said this I brought her with me."

After this nothing more was said. The evening meal was prepared, and they had supper, they also gave the girl to eat. Thereupon they took the bedsteads in and spread a mat[7] for the girl, and so they passed the night.

Adọ dosar hilok̓ setak̓ khange uni kuṛi dọ guric̓ khạclạk̓e sap̓ gọtket̓te guric̓ hạr goṛateye bọlọ gọt̓ena; adọ ona giḍi cabakate racakoe jọk̓ket̓a, dak̓koe lo ạguket̓a. Adọko mẹnet̓a, Ayọ, nui kuṛi dọ hẹc̓ caltege behaje kạmi kan! Cet̓ leka cọṅ katha menak̓tạkin. Ar uni hõko bẹṅgẹtae kana, khub mõṅjgeye ṅẹlok̓ kana. Adọ uni koṛaren eṅgat apatkin cepet̓ena, Ma nui kuṛi dọ abongebon dọhọyea, babon sẹn ocoaea. Adọ sạri ini koṛa ṅutumtege bạhu mẹnteko dọhọkedea. Adọ dosar hilok̓ ạyup̓ khon dọ mit̓ parkomre gitic̓ko hukumat̓kina. Adọ ẹn hilok̓ khon dọ mitrekin gitic̓ena, adọ sit̓ beohar lekakin kạmiket̓a, mit̓ mọnenakin.

Adọ uni kuṛiye mẹnet̓a, uni koṛae metae kana, Iạ nit dọ alaṅ dọlaṅ haṛam buḍhiyena; mit̓ din lạgit̓ dọ baṅ, jug jug bhuṅjạu lạgit̓ge jạnic̓ ayo babateko dọhọ jurikat̓laṅa. Adọ mit̓ katha kiriạkateṅ metam kana, bhalam dọhọetiṅa sẹ baṅ? Judim dọhọetiṅ khan, am ṭhen iṅ tahẹna, ar baṅkhan am ṭhen dọ ọhọṅ tahẽlena. Hẹo tọlkate dọ ọḍokok̓ hõ ạḍi moskila. Onate nitregeṅ metam kana, judim dọhọetiṅ khan iṅ rọṛa ar baṅkhan baṅ.

Adọe metadea, Ma ẹnte rọṛlem cet̓ katha kana.

Adọ uni kuṛiye mẹnket̓a, Katha dọ noa kana: jãhãn karọnte gharọṅjre eṅga apa, sẹ bọkọ boeha, sẹ haṛam buḍhi, jọtọgebon jhogṛak̓gea, alaṅ hõ hapẹn jãhãn karọntelaṅ jhogṛak̓gea, kam kaj daete cọṅ cet̓ daete cọṅ, ape herel họpọn oka dọ hạṇḍi ṅũ bulkate ạḍipe rukhet̓gea, dal hõpe dadalgea; adọ onate nitre am iṅ lạiam kantalaṅa, jãhãnak̓laṅ kạphạriạu jọkhẹnem daleṅ, sẹm kuhạuiṅ, sẹm humạgiṅ, onako dọ jọtọgeṅ sahaogetama, mẹnkhan niạ jaṅgateak̓ dọ ọhọṅ sahaoletama; inạtet̓ iṅ manakam kana; lẹk̓bẹt̓, sẹ thạk̓yạ, sẹ kokolsa jaṅgate dọ alom thạyạ lẹbẹdiṅa. Ar judi manakate hõ bam aṅjọmtiṅ ar bam batao khan, ẹnḍẹkhan oka hilok̓em thạyạyiṅ, ẹn hilok̓geṅ ọḍok calak̓a. Ma niạ katha disạ dọhọkam, ar bam dọhọetiṅ khan, ma nitrege chuṭiạṅme. Ma inạge rọṛ dọ.

Adọ uni koṛae mẹnket̓a, Acha, onaṅ disạ dọhọkak̓a; jãhã hilok̓ jaṅgate dọ bạṅ lẹbẹt̓mea.

Adọ sạri uni kuṛi arhõe mẹnket̓a, Ẹnte iṅ dọ eṅgaṅ ạpuṅ k̓õ ạḍi saṅgiṅre menak̓koa, ar am dọ ale oṛak̓ hõ bam ṅẹlakat̓a; alaṅ dọ ẹkẹn họrregelaṅ ṅapamakana, ẹnḍẹ khongem ạguakadiṅa.

Adọ unre uni koṛae mẹnket̓a, Adọ ẹnte mit̓ dhao gan hõ nạiharte dọ bam idiṅa, bam uduk̓aṅa?

---

8 The Santals have a number of baskets, named according to size and shape, and also, as here, according to use. The one here mentioned has the common bowl-shape, like practically all Santal baskets made from bambco. All cow- and buffalo-dung is collected. It is sometimes used for manuring purposes. Over large tracts in India dried cow-dung is used as and is the only fuel.

9 It must not be supposed that the proceeding here described is the ordinary Santal marriage which, when carried out according to the proper rites and ceremonials, is a very circumstantial affair. It sometimes happens that a young man will take a girl in without ceremony; more often a girl, standing in an illicit relation to a young man, will 'forcibly' enter a house to protect herself or to bring about a regular marriage. Such a girl will, on entering, touch the household utensils and act as one belonging to the house. The result will always be a 'palaver', with settling of accounts, and finally a dismissal or a regular marriage. The girl here acts something like a 'run-in' wife, as they call them, although some of the essentials are not mentioned.

10 A veiled expression for having children. The Santals carry their children riding on the left hip.

11 The expressions used refer to the different ways in which a man who has no shoes may use his foot for kicking. Santali has different words for every way.

The following morning the girl took a cow-dung basket[8] and went straight into the cattle-shed to collect the dung; having finished this and thrown the dung out, she swept the courtyard and went and fetched water. "Oh mother," they said, "this girl, she has just come, and she works like a wonder. Who knows what kind of an understanding there is between these two." Of course, they were also looking at the girl, she was very beautiful in appearance. So the young man's parents consulted together and agreed: "Let us keep this girl, we must not let her go away." And in very truth they kept the girl to be the wife of this same young man, and from the next night they ordered them to lie on the same bed. From that time they slept together and became of one mind[9].

The girl then said, that is, she spoke to the young man: "I say, now we two have become husband and wife; not for a day or two, but to live together for all time, father and mother have likely joined us together. Now there is one matter about which I speak to you most solemnly: will you do as I say or not? If you do as I say, I shall remain with you; otherwise I will never agree to remain. When one becomes tied by having to carry on the hip[10], it is also most difficult to leave. Therefore I speak out to you now; if you will do as I say, I shall speak, otherwise not."

"Well then," he said, "let me first hear what it is."

Then the girl said: "It is this I am referring to: for some reason or other father and mother, brothers and sisters, or husband and wife, that is all of us in a family will some time have a quarrel. We two will also some day, for some reason or other, start quarrelling, may be on account of the house work, or on account of some other matter. You men sometimes get drunk, and then scold something awful; you men also go so far as to beat. Therefore I already now tell you between our two selves: if at any time we have a quarrel, you may strike me, or use your fist on me, or beat me, all such things I shall put up with from you; but anything with the foot I am not standing from you. This I forbid you: trampling, or kicking with the sole of the foot, or kicking with the toes[11], you must not in any way trample on me or kick me with your foot. If you, after I have warned you, will not listen to what I have said or heed it, then the day you kick me, that day I shall leave. Please retain this in your memory; if you will not listen to me, give me free now. This is what I had to say."

"All right," the young man said, "I shall remember this; I shall never at any time kick you with my foot."

Then the girl again said: "You see, my parents are living very far away, and you have not been to our house either; we two have only just met one another on the road; from there you have brought me."

The young man answered: "Will you not then take me, if only for once, to the house of my parents-in-law? will you not let me see that?"

Adǫ unre uni kuṛiye mẹnkeťa, Iń dǫ ǫṇḍẹ khon kạhīskateń oḍokakana, ǫṇḍẹ dǫ ǫhǫgeń sẹnlena.

Adǫ inạkʼtege uni kuli ruạṛe reaḱ dǫe hiṛińkeťa. Khange adǫkin thir baṛayena.

Adǫ aghăṛ tioḱen khan ko baha sãohãkeťkina. Adǫ bǫchǫr din khangekin gidrạwana. Adǫ uni kuṛiye rophayen khan, kathae, bẹbạṛićko kisặṛena, jǫtǫ jinisge ạḍi hoeyentakoa. Adǫ onakate arhǫ̃ miťṭańkin gidrạwana, adǫ jǫtǫko tuluć ạḍi sulukgeko tahẽyena.

Adǫ ḍher dine tahẽyen khan, kathae, uni kọṛa dǫ mǫnẹ mǫnẹteye mẹnkeťa, Bhala miť din dǫ ẹṛẹ ẹṛẹte michạ michi kạphạriạu iń ẹhǫba, adǫń thạyạ gǫdea, bhalae oḍok calaḱa sẹye tahẹna.

Adǫ kathae, miť din dǫ hạṇḍiye ńũ ạguakawana, adǫ michạ michi jhogṛae ẹhǫpkeťteye thạyạ gǫťkedea. Adǫ uni bạhu kuṛi dǫ ạḍi bạṛiće raḱkeťa, mẹnkeťae, Durrẹ! am dǫ ạḍi bẹbuj hǫṛ kanam; nǫ̃ḱõeyem thạyạ gǫťkidińa, adǫm mǫkǫńadińa, iń dǫ onategem thạyạkidińa. Sei dinreń metaťmea, jańgate dǫ alom jǫṭẹdińa, mẹnkhan ińaḱ katha bam dǫhǫleťa, nǫ̃ḱõeyem jǫṭẹťkidińgea. Herel hǫpǫn ạḍi ẹṛẹpe galmaraoa. Ma adǫ in dinge am ṭhen dǫń tahẹn kana. Iń dǫń oḍok calaḱ kana, ar nukin gidrạ hǫ̃ banar dǫń idi torakina.

Adǫ uni kọṛa dǫ ceť hõ bae rǫṛ daṛeaḱ kana. Adǫ kathae, gidrại hẹokeťkina; adǫko oḍok gǫťena. Adǫ uni kọṛa dǫe bhabnayenteye ǫr ruạṛeťkoa, adǫ bako ruạṛ kana; jǫtǫ hǫṛteko ruạṛeťkore hǫ̃, bako ruạṛ kana. Adǫko mẹnkeťa, Acha, thoṛa sạńgiń sẹn ńǫ̃ḱ ocoako, adǫbon ruạṛ ạgukoa. Katha bae ańjǫmeť khanbo cekaea?

Adǫ uni kuṛiye mẹnkeťa, Aperen hǫpǫn herelge bae dǫhǫleť khan dǫń cekaea? Iń ma tahẹn hǫṛge, adǫ nui apatteťgeye bidạwadiń khan iń cekaea?

Adǫ baṛge hǫṛteye oḍok gǫťena; tala baṛge kathaeye sẹnlen khange dugur dugur jǫtǫko jol gǫťena, ać hǫ̃ ar unkin gidrạ hǫ̃.

Khange onako ńẹlkeť khan, jǫtǫ hǫṛ ạḍi bạṛićko bǫtǫrena, arko mẹnkeťa, Durrẹ! Cele kuṛibon bạhuledea? Cekate boge bae jǫmleťbon?

Adǫ uni kọṛa dǫ mǫnẹ mǫnẹte ạḍi bạṛiće bhabnayena, mẹnkeťae, Cedaḱ cǫń thạyạkede? Onategeye oḍok calaoena, ar bańkhan hutẹ̃ć ǫhǫe oḍoklena; ińgeń bạṛickeťa; onatege pạhilre besgeye metadiń tahẽkana, adǫ onkan hǫṛ ǫhǫń ńamlekoa. Adǫ uniye oḍoken khać, kathae, arhǫ̃ko rẹ̃ńgẹ̃ć ruạṛena.

Cabayena uni kọṛa reaḱ katha dǫ.

---

12 *Aghăr* is the month from the middle of November to the middle of December, often used for performing certain ceremonies.

13 See above, p. 50, note 9. A regular public ceremony is gone through.

14 The Santals live in villages, but their houses are always lying separated from each other, each homestead standing close to the village street, at the end of a field, in which maize and cold weather crops are cultivated.

15 The expression does not imply that the persons were consumed by fire. The Santals have a superstition that, in certain circumstances, bongas will emit a more or less strong light. A light seen and not recognized or understood will frequently be thought to be due to supernatural causes.

"I have come out from there, vexed in my mind," the girl said, "and am quite unwilling to go there."

Having talked so much, he forgot to question her more, and so they let the matter rest.

When the month of aghāṛ[12] came, they legalized their irregular marriage[13], and when a year had passed, they got a child. When the girl had settled down, content with her circumstances, they became awfully rich; all kinds of goods they got. Then they again had a child, and they were living happily in great peace with everybody.

After she had been living there for a long time, it came to pass that the man one day said to himself: "Well, I wonder, one day I shall find some pretext, and for fun start a quarrel and then give her a kick, I wonder whether she will leave or stay."

So one day he came home after having drunk rice-beer, he commenced, on some pretext, to quarrel and suddenly kicked her. The wife commenced to cry bitterly. "Woe, woe," she said, "you are a man without any sense; see there, you kicked me and did for me. It was therefore you kicked me. That day I told you: Don't touch me with your foot. But you have not listened to what I said; look, now you have touched me. You men are great liars. Well now then, so long I have stayed with you; I am leaving now, and these two children also I take both along with me."

The man could not say a word, and the girl took the two children on her hips, and they went out. Now the man became sorry and tried to draw them back again; but they would not return, and even when all in the house tried to persuade them to come back, they would not. So they said: "Well, let them go and get some distance off; then we shall bring them back again. If she does not listen to what we say, what can we do?"

The girl then said: "Since your son did not listen, what can I do? I am of those who remain. When the father of this child has sent me away, what can I do?"

Hereupon she went out and took the way over the fields[14]. When she reached the middle of the field in which the house was standing, they all blazed up[15], both she and her two children. When the others saw this, all of them became very frightened. "Oh, oh," they cried out, "what kind of a girl is it that we made our daughter-in-law? How is it, and how fortunate that she did not eat us."

But the young man grieved very much in his mind and said to himself: "How could I kick her? That was the cause of her leaving; otherwise she would certainly not have left. It was my fault. Why, she also told me beforehand. And now I shall certainly not get anyone like her."

When she left them, these people, it is told, again became quite poor.

The story of the young man is ended.

2. Bạijạl kọṛa reaḱ katha

Sedae jọkhẹn, kathae, mit́ṭaṅ atore Bạijạl ńutuman mit́ṭaṅ koṛae tahẹ̄kana, ar uni koṛa dọ tirio ọrọṅ ar baḱnam dọ khube bạḍae kan tahẹ̄kana. Adọ kathae, ona aṅjọmte mit́ṭaṅ boṅga kuṛiye bulạuente mit́ din dọ eskare tahẹ̄kan jọkhẹn uni kuṛi dọ Hoṛ kuṛi chinte uni lahareye sọdọrente sakame hẹheć kan. Adọ uni koṛa hō̱ uni kuṛi sẹngeye calao idiyena. Adọ kathae, uni kuṛige ọtẹye rọṛ mạṛaṅ gọt́keta, Henda peṛa, okaren kanam?

Khange uniye mẹnket́a, Niạkoren kangeaṅ; ar am dọm okaren kana?

Uni hō̱e mẹnket́a, In hōṅ niạkoren kangea.

Adọ uni koṛae mẹnket́a, Ọhọń ńẹl orometmea.

Adọ uni kuṛi hō̱e mẹnket́a, Am hō̱ cọń bań ńẹl orometme.

Adọ enka enkatege khilḍukin ẹhọṕket́a, adọkin sạrinaḱket́a, bọtọr bhaṅgaoentakina. Adọ dingekin ńapama. Adọ mit́ din dọe metadea, Dela ale oṛaḱteń idimea, inạ dọ ale oṛaḱ hō̱m ńẹl ạgukatalea. Adọe idikedea.

Adọ calaḱ calaḱte mit́ṭaṅ darharekin bọlọḱ ḳana, adọ kathae, ṭhiṭṛạ̄ḱte daḱre bọlọḱ lekae ạikaulet́a. Adọ tinre cọkin parọmket́te ḍahar ḍahartekin calaḱ kan. Adọ oṛaḱkin tioḱket́ khan, apat baret uni kuṛiko kulikedea, Nui dọ ọkọeyem ạgukedea?

Adọ uni koṛa dọ bogeteye bọtọroḱ kana. Adọ uni kuṛiye metadea, Am dọ alom bọtọ-roḱa, ọhọń ceka ocomea. Adọ duṛuṕ lạgit́ mạciko beladea, adọ onareye duṛuṕena. Ar uni kuṛi dọe lạiat́koa, Nui dọ jāwāe iń ạguakadea.

Ar kathae, bić dọko gaṇḍo kantakoa, ar kul tạruṕ dọko seta kantakoa, ar taben dọ meral sakam kantakoa, ar piṭhạ dọ gō̱ẹṭha. Ar nọtẹre koṛaren eṅgat apat dọko mẹnet́a, Aleren koṛa dọ okate cọe aṅgẹnen. Onkako mẹnet́a.

Adọ kathae, pẹ pon māhā ọṇḍẹko dọhọkedea. Adọ mit́ din dọ baretteko maraḱ sendrako riạukedea; metadeako, Delabon jāwāe, maraḱ sendra.

Adọ uni koṛa hō̱e mẹnket́a, Acha delabon.

Adọko metadea, Ma uni seta tiạgetabonme.

Adọe mẹnket́a, Ma ape baṛẹ tiạgepe, iń dọ nahāḱ birreń tiạgetabona.

Adọ sạrikọ calaoena, bir birteko sendra idiyet́a; adọ bir mucạt́re mit́ hoṛ hurut́e kuḱṭạm kana. Adọ uni koṛako metadea, Hạni haṇḍẹ, jāwāe, maraḱe ạtiń kana; ma seta tiạḱ idiyeben; pạhil dọ capat́ gọdeben, adọ seta liliạueben.

---

1 See p. 46, note 1.

2 It is a common idea with Santals that, when a man is taken away to the netherworld, the transition is made through water, the person in question being unconscious of what is happening until all is past.

3 The Santals are not alone in believing that the people of the netherworld use snakes for stools and cow-dung for bread. As to the first, it might be noted that what is here called a stool (in Santali, a *gando*) is only a flat piece of wood, generally fashioned just a little underneath, so as to leave a 'leg' or support at each end. It is not necessary to have recourse to something fantastically twisted and coiled to imagine a snake doing service as a *gando*.

4 *Taben* is parched rice pounded hard and flat. Rice made up in this way is very commonly taken along when making provision for a journey.

2. THE STORY OF THE YOUNG MAN BAIJAL

ONCE upon a time, long long ago, it is told, there was in a village a young man named Baijal, and this young man was awfully good at playing the flute and fiddling. By hearing him a bonga[1] girl was enraptured, and one day when the boy was alone, the girl appeared before him in human shape and showed herself engaged in gathering leaves. Then the young man also went towards the girl, and she, they tell, spoke first saying: "I say, friend, where do you come from?"

He answered: "I am from somewhere hereabouts; and you, where do you come from?"

The girl answered: "I am also from somewhere hereabouts," whereupon the young man said: "I am sure I don't recognize you."

Little by little they commenced to flirt and dally with each other, and ultimately they lost all fear. They got into the habit of meeting daily. One day she said to him: "Come along, I shall take you to our house; so you will also see how our home is." And she took him along.

As they were walking along, they came to a water-pool and went into the water. He felt, they tell, as if he entered the water up to the shins. Before he knew where he was, they had passed through and were walking along a road[2]. When they reached the house, the father and brothers of the girl asked her: "Who is this one that you have brought along with you?"

The young man was awfully afraid, but the girl said to him: "Don't be afraid, I shall not let anything happen to you." They placed a stool before him, and he sat down on it. Thereupon the girl told them: "This is a man I have brought to be my husband."

Now it is told that 'those people' use snakes to sit on in stead of logs; tigers and leopards are their dogs[3]; their taben[4] are meral[5] leaves, and their bread dried cow-dung.

Here on 'this side' the young man's parents say to themselves: "Our boy has been spirited away somewhere."

They tell that they kept the young man there for three to four days. Then one day the girl's brothers invited him to come with them to hunt peacocks. "Come along, brother-in-law[6]," they said, "let us go and hunt peafowls".

"Well," said the young man, "let us go."

Then they said to him: "Please lead that dog of ours along with you."

But he said: "Please, you lead him along with you. When we reach the forest, I shall take him along for us."

So they started and went through the forest hunting. Now at the end of the forest a man was occupied cutting tree stumps. "Look, brother-in-law," they said, "see that one over there, the peacock who is feeding. Do take the dog along; be quick and hit him first with something, and so set the dog on."

---

[5] *Meral* is the name of a small tree, *Phyllanthus Emblica*, L., having tiny leaves in shape and size resembling *taben*.

[6] It might be noted, that the people of the 'other side' at once recognize the relationship brought about by the action of the girl. No regular marriage is thought necessary or even possible.

Adǫ baṛkaćteye metako kana, Ukurić ho? Bań ńęl ńame kan dǫ.

Adǫko metadea, Uni ho huruťe kukťạm kan, uni kangeae marak̕ dǫ.

Adǫ uni koṛae bujhạukeťa, Judi nahăk̕le goćkedea mẹnkhan, dhorage hǫr jel dǫko jǫm ocońa. Adǫ uni koṛage seta dǫko tiạk̕ ocokedea, arko metadea, Do uni marak̕ goć ạguyetabonme.

Adǫ sạriye calaoena, adǫ kathae, bae capaṭ pạhilledea, ẹkkaltegeye liliạu gǫťadea. Khange uni hǫr dǫe sǫntǫr gǫťente ṭẹṅgoć dǫe muṭhiạu urić gǫťkeťa, adǫ jẹmǫne dǫn gǫtade, tẹmǫnge uni dǫe kuṭạm daram gǫťkedea, ẹkkalte, kathae, miť ṭaṅgaregeye kuṭạm lonḍo lonḍo gǫťkedea; arhǫe dohṛalede khangeye sumạr utạrkedea.

Khange uni koṛa dǫe ruạṛ hećente ervelko bahǫńhartetkoe metako kana, Iạ ho, marak̕ ṭhenge seta dǫe tobak̕ goć ocoyena.

Adǫko metadea, Bam capaṭ bindạr maṛańledea?

Adǫ uni koṛae mẹnkeťa, Cekań hiriń gǫťket cǫń, bạń capaṭ maṛańledea; mẹnkeťań, seta hǫ̃ maraṅgeń ńẹle kana, bań nahăk̕e daṛek̕gea jạnić? Onka mẹnkate bạń capaťledea.

Adǫko ruheť baṛakedea, adǫ oṛak̕teko ruạṛ calaoena Adǫ oṛak̕reko lạikeťa, adǫ apatteťe mẹnkeťa, Alope ruhedea, nui lelha hǫr dǫ cedak̕pe liliạu ocoyede kana? Pạhil dǫ bape uduk̕ ceťaea? Onka mẹnkateye thir ocokeťkoa.

Adǫ inạ dosar tesar khange uni koṛae mẹnkeťa, Delań iń dǫ idi oṭokańme, iń dǫń mǫkǫńena.

Adǫ unre taben ar piṭhạko moṭra ocokedea. Adǫ bana hǫrkin hijuk̕ kana; unreye metae kana, Alom bạgia jẹmǫn dingelań ńapam.

Adǫe mẹnkeťa, Ǫhǫń bạgia. Adǫ inạ darhae parǫm gǫťkadea.

Adǫ nǫtẹre hẹćkate piṭhạ taben jǫma mẹnte moṭrae raṛakeťa, adǫ kathaeye ńẹl gǫťkeť dǫ, gǫ̃eṭha kan ar taben dǫ meral sakam. Adǫ jǫtǫ ǫnḍẹgeye raṛa giḍi dapoṛkaťa. Adǫ oṛak̕re sẹnkate gate koṛakoe lạiako kana, noako jǫtǫ kathae lạikeťa.

Mẹnkhan ẹnre hǫ̃ bakin bạgileťa, tahẹ̃yengeakin; gidrạwanakin barea. Ar atore lagrẹ̃ko ẹnẹć khan, uni dǫe hijuk̕gea, unkin gidrạ hǫ̃e ạgu darakingea; adǫ ạgukate ụni koṛawak̕ parkomrege unkin gidrạ dǫe gitićkakina ar ẹnẹće calak̕a; ẹnẹć mǫkǫńkateko calaoenge.

Adǫ miť din dǫ uni kuṛiye mẹnkeťa, Iạ, amko bạhuam kana, adǫ pạhil pǫrthǫm kuṛi gidrạko hoelen khan dǫ, iń barẹ ńumeńme, iń dǫ nonkawańa.

Adǫ sạri uni koṛako bạhuadea, ẹnre hǫ̃, kathae, kuṛi hijuk̕ dǫ bae bạgileťa. Arhǫ̃ onkage miť dhao lagrẹ̃ ẹnẹć jǫtǫ eṅga hǫpǫnko hẹćlena; adǫ onkage ẹnẹć mǫkǫńkate

---

7 Such behaviour is not deemed specially offensive. It is rather common with newly married Santal girls who wish to pay a visit to their parents. It may, of course, also be an expression signifying that one has done with something.

8 *Lagrẹ̃* is the name of a Santal dance, the one most commonly used when the rites and rules of ceremonies do not prescribe other dances. The girls form a line, catching hold of each other, and move slowly backwards and for. wards and gradually round in a circle. The men, always only a few at a time, keep it going, jumping and beating the drum in front of the women. The women generally sing some song at a lagrẹ̃ melody. The way

Pretending not to see him, he says to them: "Where? I am not able to catch sight of him."

"He over there," they said, "he who is cutting tree stumps, he is the peacock."

The young man then understood, and said to himself: "If we now kill this man, they will surely make me eat human flesh." However, they made the young man lead the dog along and said to him: "Now kill and bring us that peacock."

So he, truth to tell, went along; but he did not first throw anything at the man, he egged the dog on at once. Thereby the man became watchful, he grasped his axe tightly, and just as the dog jumped at him, he met him with a blow; with one single blow of the axe he struck him insensible, and when he gave him one more, he finished him entirely.

The young man thereupon returned to his brothers-in-law and said to them: "I say, there with the peacock the dog was pecked to death."

"Did you not then," they said, "first throw anything to fell him to the ground?"

"Somehow or other," the man answered, "I forgot that; I did not first throw anything at him. I said to myself that the dog also looked large in my eyes, and that he would likely manage. This was the reason that I did not try to hit him."

So they scolded him and returned home. When they reached there they told their tale, and the father said: "Don't scold him; why do you let this fool egg the dog on? Ought you not first to show him how to act?" Speaking in this way he silenced them.

Two or three days after this had happened, the young man said: "Come along, take me back; I have had enough of it[7]."

They let him make up a bundle of taben and bread, and the young man and the girl both started, and he said to her: "Don't quit, let us meet daily." And she said: "Certainly, I shall not leave off," whereupon she took him past the water-pool.

When he had reached this side, he opened the bundle to eat taben. But when he looked at it, he saw it was cow-dung, and the taben was meral leaves. So he opened it all and threw the stuff away then and there. Having arrived home, he told his chums everything. Still they did not leave each other, the boy and the girl continued to live together and got two children. When they had a dance in the village, the girl would also come and bring the two children along. When she brought these, she was in the habit of laying them on the young man's bed and then, she went to the dance. When the dancing was over, they all departed.

One day the girl said: "I hear they are arranging to have you married. When your first girl is born to you, name her after me, please. This must be done for me."

Now they actually had the young man married; still the bonga girl did not leave off coming. So it happened that all of them, mother and children, once came to dance l a g r e[8].

---

of dancing may be decent, but is often quite the opposite. This dance gives the two sexes an opportunity of meeting and is the occasion of much immorality.

calakko mẹneta, ar uni koṛa dọ bae sẹn ocoako kana, ọr ruạṛetkoae. Adọ bako bataoet khane siń ẹsẹtketkoa, are metako kana, Alope calaka, nọnḍẹge tahẹnpe jọtọ họṛ, mit ṭhengebon tahẹna.

Adọ uni kuṛi dọe mẹneta, Ale dọ ọhọle tahẽlena; nenka ale dọle hijuk sẹnokgea. Mẹn, ale dọ sẹn ocoaleme, alom ẹsẹt baṛalea.

Adọ bae aṛakako kante tinre cọń, kathae, cal sẹn jalat julutko rakapente kat ṭhen khonko parọmena, adọ kathae, simạ simạte jọtọge bogeteko jol calaoena.

Khange ẹn hilok khon uni koṛa dọe bọtọrena; adọ uni tuluće bạgi utạrketa. Adọ kuṛi gidrạko hoyokre hõ, uni ńume reak dọ bae mẹn baṛaea. Khange eṭakkoko ńumketkoge. Khange uni gidrại goćenge; tin dhaoko hoyok, un dhaoko gọć horaka. Adọ dak sunumreko ńam ạguadea, adọko kulikedea, adọe hẽkketa, adọ tin utạrko ńumledea, tọbẹ uniren gidrạko tahẽlena. Ọnẹ anẹć Bạijạl koṛa reak katha dọ cabayena.

3. Miṭṭań boṅga koṛa reak katha

Sedae jọkhẹn, kathae, miṭṭań bir ḍuṅgri dhiri dander ṭhen miṭṭań cạṭạnire uni boṅga dọ dinge ḍubạ sunum ar nạkić, ạrsi aenọme oḍokkaka, ar oka hilok oka hilok dọ sindur hõe oḍokkaka. Adọ jãhãege birteko calak maejiu dọ jọtọgeko ńẹl ńama, ar hẹrẹl họpọnko calaoena mẹnkhan, kathae, bako ńẹl ńama.

Adọ onka dingeko ńẹl khan, adọ kuṛiko dọ onakote nạkijok, aenọmokko pọrtọnketa, ar sunum hõko ọjọga ar ạrsite hõko ńẹloka. Adọ onkate dingeko pạrkạuena; adọ birteko calak khan, pạhil dọ ọndẹgeko sẹn pạhiloka.

Adọ onkako hewayen khan dọ, kathae, mit dhao dọ ẹkẹn kuṛi kuṛikoge mõṛẽ họṛ birteko riạu calaoena. Adọ ona dhiri ṭhenge ẹn hilok hõko sẹn pạhilena, adọ onkage nindara leka

---

[9] See p. 52, note 15.

[10] Any disease which cannot be cured in a 'reasonable' time, and an untimely death, will generally be thought to be due to the influence of inimical powers, bongas or witches. To ascertain what the cause is, the Santals resort to divination. An *ojha*, that is, a medicine-man, is asked to do this for them. He takes two *sal*-leaves with prominent veins, and having rubbed oil here and there on one leaf, he says that such a part of the leaf is for disease, and such a part for witches, for bongas, and so on, then he covers the first leaf with the second one, salutes, and, muttering a mantar, puts the leaves on the ground. After a short while he takes them up again, salutes and removes the covering leaf; after having scrutinized the leaf, he announces the result. It is unnecessary to say that the *ojha* arranges the result, and that he does it according to what he understands is the common opinion of those who have engaged him.

To be fully sure, the people concerned will consult a number of ojhas and also take other precautions to avoid doing anybody an injustice. Most Santals have at the present day lost their belief in this kind of divination; still it is a matter of nearly daily occurrence.

and when they had done dancing, they wanted to go as usual; but the young man was not willing to let them go; he tried to pull them back, and when they would not listen to him, he shut them up in the house and said to them: "Don't go away; remain here, all of you. We shall live together, all of us."

But the girl answered: "We can certainly not remain here; we shall come and go, as we have done. Take care, let us go; don't attempt to block the way for us."

As he still would not let them go, they suddenly, it is told, blazed up[9] and rose towards the roof and passed out at the top of the wall. Thereupon they all of them went away in a blaze along the border of the field.

From that day the boy became frightened and left off having anything to do with the girl. When a girl was born to him, he did not say anything of naming the bonga girl either, but named other persons. The child, however, died. So often as a girl was born, so often the child died. Then they consulted the oil-oracle[10] for him and questioned him, whereupon he confessed the truth. First when they had named the bonga girl, his children would live. That is the end of the story of Baijal.

3. THE STORY OF A BONGA MAN

ONCE upon a time long long ago, they tell, there was a bonga who was in the habit of bringing daily a lot of oil and combs, mirrors and eye-paint[1] out and placing all this on a flat rock near a rock-cave in a forest-covered hill; now and then he also brought some sindur[2] out. Now all women who passed there on their way to the forest, caught sight of these things; but if any man passed that way, he never caught sight of it, people tell.

As the girls saw this every day, they commenced to comb themselves with the combs and to apply the eye-paint; they also rubbed themselves in with the oil and had a look at themselves in the mirror. In this way they, day by day, got into the habit of doing it; when they went to the forest, they always first went to this place.

When they had got into this habit, it is told, it once happened that five of them, only girls, agreed to go to the forest together. Also this time they went first to the rock mentioned, and according to their habit they also that day combed themselves. When they

---

1 What is here called eye-paint is a kind of lamp-black, very frequently used by Santal women to blacken their eyelids. The Santals have an idea, that bongas may bring out things to be found by human beings. As an example the following may be mentioned. The writer has among other things been collecting stone-beads, found in the ground, likely in old burial places. When once going to such a place, he was told it was quite useless to go that particular day, because it was only on Thursdays that the bongas brought these things out 'for market.'

2 *Sindur* is the red lead which is so extensively used by (the Hindus and also) the Santals for religious purposes. It is used in connexion with their spirit worship; the essential part of the marriage ceremony — except with a few of their subsepts — is that the bridegroom puts streaks of *sindur* on the forehead of the bride.

ẹn hiloḱ hõko nạkijoḱ kana; adọ nạkić baṛakateko bereṭena. Adọ miṭṭaṅ kuṛi dọ, kathae, cekakote cọe tayọmen, bae nạkić hoṭlen, adọ onko ponea dọko calao gọṭena.

Uni dọe tayọmen khange bonga koṛa dọe oḍok gọṭente dea sẹn khon hape hapete hẹćkateye haṛup gọṭkedea. Khange uni kuṛi dọe bọtọrente bogeteye họhọketa. Adọ onko gate kuṛi hijuḱtege, kathae, ona dhiri danderteye haṛup aderkedea; thoṛa lạgiṭ bako jhuṭiạu tioḱledea. Adọ onko kuṛi dọ ạḍi baṛićko bhabnayena, arko mẹneṭa, Ma boṅga koṛa, aṛaḱ gọṭkaeme, baṅkhan nahāḱ oṛakre alege ạḍi baṛićko ruheṭlea. Niạ dhao dọ aṛaḱkaeme.

Adọ uni boṅga koṛae mẹnkeṭa, Do, ape dọ ruạṛ calaḱpe, nui dọ ọhọń aṛaḱlea; nui dọ iṅgeń bạhuyea.

Adọ khange miṭṭẹn kuṛiko kolkadea arko mẹn gọṭadea, Do, am dọ sẹnkate nui gate kuṛiren eṅgat apat lạiakome, Aperen kuṛi dọ hana phalna dhiri danderren boṅga koṛae aṅgẹnkedetapea. Onage lạiape lạgit iń dọń hẹćakana. Ar adọm họr dọ ọnḍẹge menaḱkoa; bae aṛaḱede kana, onate iń dọko kol gọtkadiṅa, do lạiakome mẹnte.

Adọ kathae, inạḱtege uni boṅga koṛa dọ dhiri kapaṭṭe ona duạr dọe siń ẹsẹṭketa. Ar uni kuṛiren eṅgat apat dọ kạumạu garja barjakin ńir hẹćena ona dhiri dander ṭhen; adọkin kuliketḱoa, Ceṭ lekate nui dọe aṅgẹnkedea?

Adọko mẹnkeṭa, Nọnḍẹge nạkić, ạrsi, aenọmle ńamketa; adọ ḍubạ sunum ọjọḱkatele nạkić baṛayena; adọ nui aperen kuṛi dọ ceka lekate cọe tayọmen, adọe haṛup ader gọṭkedea.

Adọ onko gate kuṛikoge bogetekin ruheṭ baṛaketḱoa; adọ ẹnte onko ceṭko mẹna? Thir doroḱenako, ceṭ hõ bako rọṛleṭa. Adọ eṅgatteṭe raḱkeṭa; adọko sereńaḱa raḱ sereń:

Ḍubạ sunumem nọjọḱkeṭ na, mạ̃i na,
Kundạr nạkićem nạkićen na, mạ̃i na,
Dẹ mạ̃i na, nonḍoṅ hijuḱme.

Adọ kuṛiye rọṛ ruạṛketa:

Dhiri siṅe siṅkidiń, nayo,
Dhiri kawaṛe kawaṛkidiń, nayo,
Do nayo, ruạṛjoṅme.

Adọ apattẹte raḱkeṭa:

Ḍubạ sunumem nọjọḱkeṭ na, mạ̃i na,
Kundạr nạkićem nạkićen na, mạ̃i na,
De mạ̃i na, nonḍoṅ hijuḱme.

Adọ uni hõ onka lekae rọṛ ruạṛadea:

Dhiri siṅe siṅkidiń, baba,
Dhiri kawaṛe kawaṛkidiń, baba,
Do baba, ruạṛjọṅme.

Adọ kathaeko ruạṛ calaoena jọtọ họr.

had done so they rose to go. Somehow or other one of the girls fell behind; she was not quick enough combing herself, and four of them started going.

When this girl fell behind, the bonga man came out at once, and going stealthily up to her from behind, he suddenly threw his arms round her. The girl was frightened and called out loudly; but before her girl companions could come, the bonga had carried the girl in his arms into the rock-cave. They barely missed to catch hold of her hair. The girls became exceedingly sorry and called out: "Please, bonga boy, set her free; otherwise they will scold us awfully at home. Please, set her free this time."

But the bonga man said: "You return home. I will certainly not set the girl free. I shall make the girl my wife."

There was nothing for it, the other girls sent one of their number and instructed her what to do: "You go to the parents of our girl friend and tell them: The bonga man living in such and such a rock-cave has spirited your daughter away. I have come to tell you this. Some people are there on the spot; but he will not set her free; therefore they have sent me to tell you."

In the meantime the bonga man closed the entrance with a stone door. The parents of the girl came running, crying and howling, up to the entrance of the cave, and asked the other girls, how the bonga had spirited their daughter away.

"Here," they answered, "we found combs, mirrors and eye-paint, and after we had rubbed us in with the liquid oil flowing all over, we combed ourselves. Then somehow or other your daughter fell behind, and he threw his arms round her and carried her in."

They scolded her girl companions all round; but what could these say? They kept quiet and did not say a word. Thereupon the mother of the girl cried and sang (here they sing the following lamentation song):

You rubbed yourself in with the oil flowing all over, my girl,
You combed yourself with the comb, my girl,
Please, my girl, come out.

The girl answered:

He shut me up in the rock, mother,
He imprisoned me in a rock prison, mother,
Do, mother, return home.

Then the father cried:

You rubbed yourself in with the oil flowing all over, my girl,
You combed yourself with the comb, my girl,
Please, my girl, come out.

The girl answered him also in the same way:

He shut me up in the rock, father,
He imprisoned me in a rock prison, father,
Do, father, return home.

Thereupon all of them went away home.

Adọ inạ tayọm khange kạkit kakatkin hẹćena, adọ unkin hõ onka lekakin rakketa; adọ unkin hõ onkageye rọr ruạraťkina; adọ unkin hõkin ruạrena. Adọ mamọt hatọmtẹttikinkin hẹćena, adọ unkin hõ onkage. Adọ ẹkẹ ẹkẹte jọtọ peṛako hẹć cabayena; adọ onkageko rakketre hõ bae ọdoklena.

Adọ sẹsre, kathae, barettẹť sadọmre dẹćkateye hẹćena, adọ uni hõ onkageye rakketa, ar uni hõ onkageye rọr ruạradea. Ceť lekan sadọm cọe tahẽkantae, adọ uni sadọme puski gọťadea; adọ uni sadọm dọe ạcur gọťente ona dhiri silpińe phandaleťa sẹ, kathaeye phanda jhić gọťketa, adọ arhõe ńẹlkeť dọ bhitrire dhiri kawaṛ menak; adọ ona dọ bae jhić daṛeaťa. Khange adọkin ruạṛ calaoena, adọ bogeyena.

Adọ kathae, tahẹn tahẹntege tinạk din badre cọń uni kuṛiye mẹnketa, Iạ, dher din iń hoeyena; delań ayo babateko miť dhao ganlań hiri ạgukakoa.

Adọ sạri uni jãwãetẹť boṅga koṛa hõe mẹnketa, Acha, ẹndẹkhan gapalań calaka.

Adọ sạri sandesok lạgitkin juṛạu baṛaketa, piṭhạ ar tabenkoe sajao ocokedea, adọkin calaoena. Adọ sẹtẹrkate besge ạiso baisoko atań daramkeťkina, mạci parkọmko belaťkina ar besgeko beohar baṛaketa. Adọ ẹn hilok dọko dọhọketkina. Adọ ona idiak sandes dọ kathaeko ńẹlketa, piṭhạ dọ gõẹṭha kan ar taben dọ meral sakam kan. Adọ uni kuṛiko metae kana, Dela sẹ mãi, nọtẹ hẹćlenme. Adọ oṛak sẹn họhọ aderkateko udukae kana.

Adọe mẹnketa, Baṅa, ayo, piṭhạ ar tabengeń sajaoleťa, adọ cekate cọń nonkayen, ona dọ ọhọń mẹn daṛelea; baṅkhan piṭhạ ar tabengeń sajaoleťa.

Adọ apattẹťe mẹnketa, Acha cekaeam? Bogeyena. Ma alope rọr baṛaea, thir dapọṛkokpe, ar baṅkhan nahãkpe bhiṛkạukina; adọ hikri hõ ọhọkin hẹćlena.

Adọ sạri sanam họrko thir baṛayena. Adọ uni barettẹť dọ landa sạgai iạte uni boṅga koṛa tuluć dọ khube gateyena ar khube galmarao kana; emanteak phukṭikin galmarao kana. Adọko peṛa baṛaketkina, khubko marjạtketkina.

Adọ dosar hilokko bidạketkina. Adọ onakin calak jọkhẹnge uni kuṛiren barettẹť dọe mẹnketa, Iń hõ aben sãote atra dhur ńẹl gogọť dọń calakgea.

---

[3] It is not uncommon that Santals, when going on a visit to friends, take some kind of gifts with them for those to whom they go, food of some kind and other things, for instance, *sal*-twig-toothbrushes to people living far away from the *sal*-forests.

[4] The Santals have very little in the way of furniture. They sit on anything serviceable. Generally they have a couple of *gandos* (see p. 54, note 3) and one or two *macis* (i. e. square wooden frames on four low legs, with stringed seats), besides bedsteads. These last ones are rectangular wooden frames on four legs with a string bottom, woven in a peculiar way. When not in actual use, the beds are, generally, raised on one side and placed somewhere out of the way. When visitors come, it is the common custom to place a bedstead for them to sit on. It might be remarked that the 'furniture' here mentioned is all made by the Santals themselves. All do not know to string a *mạci*, but a man who could not string a bedstead would be considered a dunce.

[5] When visitors come, they are not expected to remain, unless invited to do so. When relatives come to pay a visit, they generally manage to come in the afternoon, stay next day and then leave early the following morning. To stay longer, if not specially invited, would not be considered good form. Often, of course, the visit is shorter, as here.

[6] Se p. 42, notes 4 & 5.

Some time afterwards the girl's paternal uncle and aunt came and cried in the same way; but these she also answered in the same manner, and these two also went away. Then her maternal uncle and aunt came and acted in the same way and got the same answer. Then, one after the other, all her relatives came; but although they also cried in the same way, she did not come out.

At last her brother came, riding a horse. He also cried in the same way, and him also she answered in the same manner. What kind of a horse it now was that he had, the horse suddenly gave him a hint. The horse turned quickly round and gave that stone door a kick so strong that he kicked the door open; but alas, he saw that there was inside still a rock fence, and this he was unable to open. So he and his horse returned home, and the matter was left as it was.

The girl consequently remained; then after some time, goodness knows how long a time it was, she said: "Look here, it is a long time since I came; come along, let us go on a visit, for once anyhow, to my parents."

Her husband, the bonga man, also agreed. "Well," he said, "we shall go to-morrow then."

So they prepared some presents of food[3] to take along; he told her to pack cakes and taben, and so they went. When they reached the place, her relatives received them well and friendly, placed a stool and a bedstead[4] before them to sit on and behaved in a fine manner. That day they asked them to remain[5]. When they looked at the gifts of food brought, look and behold, the cakes are cow-dung and the taben meral[6] leaves. "Please, my girl," they called to their daughter, "come here a moment." And calling her into the house they showed it to her.

"Oh no, mother," she said, "it was cakes and taben that I wrapped up. However this has happened, I am sure I cannot say. Anyhow, I certainly packed cakes and taben."

"All right," the father said, "what can you do? It is all right. Please, don't talk of it; keep quiet, can't you; otherwise you will presently scare them away, and then they will never again come here on a visit."

So they, all of them, did not say anything more. Now the girl's brother, on account of the laughing relationship[7], made great friends with the bonga man and kept the talk going; they were constantly cracking jokes. They entertained them and feasted them exceedingly well.

The next day they bade them farewell. When they were starting, the girl's brother said: "I will also go half-way along with you to see you off."

---

[7] The relationship between certain relatives, specially brothers-in-law and sisters-in-law, a man and his elder brother's wife, or his wife's younger sisters, further certain nephews and nieces and their uncle, and grandparents and grandchildren, is called *landa sagai*, laughing relationship, which means that such persons may laugh and jest and be intimate with one another. They are not supposed to stand on their dignity.

Adokin menketa, Bogege endekhan. Ado uni kora do kapiye oyo potomketa, ado unkin tayom tayomteye calak kana. Ado uni kuri doe laha akana, ar ona tayomre bonga kora menaea, ar ona tayomre do uni hor kora atra dhure ńel gotkakin kana.

Ado barge mucat then mittan bir tahẽkana, ado ona bir thenge uni bonga kora do, kathae, tayom sen khone mak oco gotena, ekkalte hotokgeye mak topak gotkettaea. Ado uni miserate metadea, Dela na, ruarme; jāwāe doń gockedea. Ado sari benget acurkateye ńelkede doe mak bindar akade. Khangekin ruarena. Ado thora sangiń hec ńokkatekin benget ruarket dokin ńelket, akin tayomte bohok do gudrau hijuk kan!

Khange botorte markin dar — ado ekkalte ako oraktekin ńir hecena; ado onde habicge bohok hõ gudrau hecena. Khange ona botorte unkin do oraktekin ńir boloyena, ado bohok hõ orakte gudrau boloyena. Ado dakka lagit culhare sengelko jol akat tahẽkana, adoko jhũkente ona bohok do culha sengelreko hotor khadle gotkata; ado lo rongoyena. Ado onakate adiko raskayena, menketako, Bhageledeam, ia bongage, engate khubledeam.

Ado inakate āt lo din gange janić hoelena, ado uni kuri bohok haso ehopkedea; ado ranadere hõ bae beslena, ina hasotegeye gocena; adoko menketa, Nui kuri do jāwāetetgeye idikedea, unige bae arakledea, onategeye gocena, ar bankhan hutec ohoe goclena. Ado eneko rapakkedea, uniakko kaj koromketa.

Ado cabayena uni kuri reak katha do, in marangea.

4. Mittan kada gupi kora reak katha

Sedae jugre, kathae, mittan kora kadae gupi kan tahẽkana, ar uni kora do danguageye tahẽkana. Ado mittan gada sodok senre thora thuri dak tahẽkana. Ado din hilokge mittan enga setae ńelea, thik tikin jokhen khange uni seta do ona gada sodok sengeye calaka. Ado uni korae mena, Bhala nui seta doe okoeren kan bań? Ar din hilok noa sodok sengeye calak kana; bhala noa sodokre do cet lagite calaka? Bhala mit din do tārakkateń ńelea.

Ado onka menkate kathae, mit din doe tārakena, ado kathae, en hilok hõ tikin khange uni enga seta doe hec gotente ona gada sodok sengeye calaoena. Adoe calaoen khan, uni

---

[8] The battle-axes (of some five or six different shapes) are now-a-days not very common. They are at the present time used for sacrificial purposes.

[9] See p. 52, note 14. [10] See p. 47, note 5.

[11] A headache of the kind here mentioned is very commonly believed to be due to supernatural causes. It is not unusual to hear that dead persons call for some living relatives to follow them. The writer remembers the following: An old woman, who was commonly believed to be, and for that matter also acknowledged herself to be, a witch, died. When she was being burnt, she raised one arm and one leg up. This was considered ominous. A short time afterwards two of her grandchildren died. The village people firmly believed that the old women had wanted these children to follow after her.

[12] The funeral rites and ceremonies are circumstantial, numerous and obligatory.

"That is quite well, then," said they. The brother took a battle-axe[8] and wrapped it up in a cloth and walked behind those two. The girl was walking in front, behind her was the bonga man, and in the rear the young Santal, seeing them off half-way.

At the end of the field in which the house was standing[9], there was a forest, and there in that forest the bonga man, they tell, was cut from behind; he (i. e. the Santal) slashed his neck through and his head off in one stroke. Thereupon he said to his sister: "Come along, girl, return home. I have killed your husband." When she looked back, she saw him; he had in very truth cut him down. So they went back. When they had come a short distance, they looked back and saw, behold, the head came rolling after them.

O my, they were frightened and started running all they could, and ran straight home; but even there the head came rolling along. Then, still more frightened, they ran inside the house; but the head also came rolling in. Now they had lighted a fire in the fire-place to cook food, and plucking up courage they poked the head into the burning fire, so it was burnt to cinders. So they became very glad: "You gave him his deserts," they said, "that unspeakable bonga; dash it[10], you did him exceedingly well."

After this, it was perhaps eight or nine days afterwards that it happened, then the girl got a headache, and although they applied medicine, she did not recover; she died from that headache[11]. "The husband," they said, "has taken this girl away; it was he who would not let her off. Therefore she died; otherwise she would certainly not have died." So they cremated her and performed the usual rites and ceremonies on her account[12].

So the story of that girl is ended. It is thus much.

4. THE STORY OF A BOY WHO HERDED BUFFALOES

ONCE upon a time in the old days, it is told, a young man was herding buffaloes. He was not as yet married. Now there was a little water in a river-bed[1]. Here he daily saw a bitch; exactly at noon every day this dog was in the habit of going down into this river-bed. "I wonder," the young man was saying to himself, "whom this dog belongs to. She goes every day down into this river-bed. Whatever does she go down there for? Well, some day I shall watch and see."

Intent on this, he one day kept watch, and that day also the bitch came and went straight towards the river-bed. When she reached there, the young man kept his eyes open to see what the dog would do. Having this in his mind, the young man remained quiet.

---

[1] Buffaloes are always herded not far from water. It seems to be a necessity for them to lie some time in water daily; here the herdsman rubs and washes them.

koṛa dọ tan mane ńeńẹl kana, bhala nui seta dọ ceṫe cekaea. Adọ kathae, onka mẹnkate uni koṛa dọe thir akana. Adọ uni seta dọ ona sọdọḱre bọlọkate ona seta hoṛmọ dọe bọćkaṫa; adọe umoḱ kana. Adọ un jọkhẹne ńẹle kana, hoṛ hō hoṛ boṅga hō boṅga, hankae ńẹloḱ kana.

Adọ kathaeye ńẹl hapekadegea; ceṫ hō bae rọṛ sạdeleṫa. Adọe um baṛa mọkọńen khan dọ ona seta hartaregeye bọlọyena. Adọ seta yente oṛaḱteye calaḱ kana.

Adọ sạṅgiń ńọ̄ḱe calaoen khan, kathae, uni koṛa dọe bereṫente uni setageye pańja idikedea. Adọe mẹneṫa, Bhala nui seta dọe ọkọeren kana ar oka oṛaḱreye bọlọḱa, ọkọe torań ńẹl bọlọ oṭokaea. Adọ onka mẹnkate sạriye pańja idikedeteye ńẹl bọlọ oṭokadea Adọ hoṛe kulikeṫkoa, Henda họ, bhala nui seta dọe ọkọeren kan bań? Behaj jute ńẹloḱ kana. Iń hō nonkan setań ńamleko khan dọń ạsulkekoa.

Adọ onko hoṛko mẹnkeṫa, Nui seta dọe phalnaren kana. Adọ inạye suhikeṫ khan uni koṛa dọe ruạṛ hẹćena.

Adọ kathae, ẹn sermage uni koṛaren bạhuko ńam baṛayeṫkoa. Adọ uni koṛae mẹnkeṫa, Iń dọ hoṛ kuṛi dọ bań bạhukoa; iń dọ seta kuṛigeń bạhukoa. Khange adọ ạdi baṛićko landawadea. Adọ ẹnre hōe mẹneṫa, Iń dọ seta kuṛipe bạhuań khan dọń dọhọkoa; ar bańkhan dọ bań dọhọkoa.

Adọ onka jide rọṛkeṫ khanko mẹnkeṫa, Nui koṛare dọ seta jivige menaḱ cọń ceṫ cọń, onategе hoṛ dọ bae khusiako kante setageye ńam kana.

Adọ eṅgat apatkin mẹnkeṫa, Acha, ẹṇḍẹkhan setagebon ạgukoa.

Adọ uni koṛae mẹnkeṫa, Hana atote calaḱpe, uni phalna hoṛren eṅga seta menaea. Uni ńẹl ạguyepe ar kulikope. Iń do uniregeń khusi akana; ma unigebon ạguyea.

Adọ sạriko calaoenteko ńẹlkedea, ar uni hoṛ hōko kulikedea. Adọ uni hoṛ hō ạdi baṛiće landakeṫa, ar gọńako reaḱ ạdi khulạsateye hẹ̄ḱaṫkoa.

Adọ bapla reaḱko oramkeṫa. Adọ sanam sạhi juhi ṭhiken khanko mạṇḍwakeṫa, adọ baṛiạtoḱko calaoena. Adọ uni seta kuṛigeko bapla ạgukedea. Adọ onkage baret lumtiko hẹćena; adọ um naṛkakateko bidạyena.

---

2 A very common expression in Santali, the meaning being that the person in question is exceedingly beautiful, more so than is ordinarily found. It is about equivalent to 'a goddess in human shape'.

3 It might be noted, that the Santali word hoṛ, besides meaning a human being, also means a Santal. They call themselves so when asked which race they belong to.

4 The idea of transmigration is not indigenous among the Santals and not by any means commonly taken up by them; but one may meet among them speculations like what is told here. If something abnormal or monstruous is met with in some person, they may be heard attempting to explain it by supposing that the soul of an animal, having naturally characteristics similar to those observed, has entered the person.

5 A marriage is with the Santals a very circumstantial affair. The two most concerned are generally those least consulted. When a man thinks that his boy ought to get a wife, he engages a go-between, who finds out where a suitable party may be, whereupon the two families commence negotiations, the bride-price is fixed, and the engagement is made public. Small gifts are exchanged, both sides feast each other and so on, until a day for the marriage ceremony is fixed. This is regularly performed in the house of the bride. The bridegroom goes there, followed by a number of relatives and friends.

When the bitch had entered that river-bed, she took off her dog's body and had a bath. During this he was looking at her; like a human being and at the same time a spirit[2], thus she was in appearance.

He only looked at her quietly, but did not utter a single word. When she had done bathing, she entered her dog's skin, became a dog again and went homeward.

When the dog had gone some distance away, the young man got up and followed after her. He said to himself: "I wonder whose dog this one is, and which house she will enter. I shall at once follow and see her go in." And intent on this he really followed and saw the dog enter a house. He thereupon asked the people there: "I say, I wonder whoever is the owner of this dog. She is looking marvellously beautiful. If I could also get such dogs, I should like to keep them."

"This dog belongs to such and such a person," they replied. Having ascertained this, he returned home.

Now it so happened that the young man's people that very same year were seeking a wife for him, and the young man said: "I shall not marry any human[3] girl, I will marry a dog-girl." They laughed at him very much, but he still said: "If you bring me a dog-girl for a wife, I shall take her; and if not, I shall not marry at all."

As he persisted in talking in this way, they thought by themselves: "This boy must certainly have a dog's soul[4]; therefore he does not like human beings and wants a dog."

His parents then said: "Well and good, let us so bring a dog."

The young man then said: "Go to that village over there; such and such a man has a female dog. Go and have a look at her and ask them. I am pleased with her; let us bring her."

So they really went and had a look at the dog, and asked the owner for her. He also laughed uproariously, and when they asked him to give the dog in marriage, he agreed with the greatest pleasure.

Thereupon they made the necessary preliminaries for the ceremony, and when all negotiations were settled[5], they erected the marriage-shed[6] and started for the celebration. They performed the ceremony[7] and brought the girl-dog off. The representatives of her family also came along, and after they had bathed and had washed their hair, they were sent away home[8].

---

6 At each marriage a m a ṇ ḍ w a is erected in the court-yard of the parents. Some poles are fixed in the ground round a small square; rafters placed horizontally form the roof, on which a number of branches with fresh leaves is placed, giving sufficient shadow. Here the public marriage-ceremonies are mostly performed.

7 The binding part of a Santal marriage is the s i n d r ạ d a n. The bride is lifted up in a wide basket in which she is sitting. The bridegroom rides on the shoulder of a man and being taken close to the bride he five times puts a streak of *sindur*, red lead, on her forehead.

8 The text is not quite clear, whether the relatives are dogs or the dog's owner and friends. The narrator has informed me that the bridal party consisted of human beings only, that is, in his opinion.

Adǫ khange uni seta dǫ uni koṛa tulućgeko gitićkadea. Adǫ onkage ḍher din dhạbić miťrekin gitićena. Adǫ kathae, uni seta dǫ ńindạ khange ona seta hǫṛmǫ khon oḍokkate bahreteye calaḱa. Adǫ kathae, onae cią ṭhikkedea.

Adǫ miť din dǫ ęrę ęrę baṛkaćteye jạpiť laha gǫťketa. Adǫ uni kuṛi dǫ seta hǫṛmǫ khon oḍokkate calaḱe mẹneť tahẽkana. Adǫ kathae, un jǫkhẹn geye hạruṕ gǫťkedete ona seta harta dǫ culhạ sẹṅgẹlreye khanjǫ gǫťkaťa, adǫ jǫtǫ lǫ rǫṅgǫyena.

Adǫ khange uni seta dǫe hǫrena, adǫ unreko ńẹle kan dǫ, hǫr hõ hǫr boṅga hõ boṅgageye ńẹloḱ kana. Adǫ khange sanam hǫr ạdiko khusiyena, adǫ uni koṛa ạdiko sarhaokedea.

Adǫ uni koṛaren bạhu ńẹlte uni koṛaren gate koṛae mẹnketa, Iń hõ eṅgate setageń bạhukoa. Nui koṛa setae bạhuledete nonkan mõńj bạhui ńawana, tǫbẹ tǫ iń hõ setageń bạhukoa.

Adǫ sạri uni koṛa hõ seta bạhukogeye huṛsoketa, adǫ sạri seta bạhugeko siṛiketkote bapla reaḱko oramketa, adǫko manḍwaketa. Adǫ sunum sasaṅko ǫjǫge jǫkhẹn hõ, kathae, bogeteye garjao, ar sindrạ dan jǫkhẹn hõ bogeteye garjao. Adǫ kathae, ẹnre hõ enka garjao tulućgeko ạgukedegea. Adǫ kathae, nǫnḍẹ hõ onkageye garjao, adǫ jǫrmǫṭgeko sunum sasaṅketkina. Adǫ baretkoko bidạketko khan, bogeteye daṛ, baṅgeye tahẹn. Adǫ uni koṛageko metadea, Ma ya, hạni toṛa bạhui dạreťtama, do sumạrem.

Adǫ kathae, rukạṛe calaoen khan, bogeteye garjaoeť ar sǫjhẹ gẹgẹrgeye chuṭạuḱ kan. Adǫ khangeye ikạ dapoṛkadea. Adǫ khange bae ruạṛ daṛeade khan, bogeteko landawadea; adǫ uni koṛa dǫ lajaote ceť hõ bae rǫṛleta. Adǫ inạ ursiń bạrsiń khange uni koṛa dǫ lajaoteye phạsi gǫćena.

Cabayena katha dǫ, in maraṅgea.

5. Gupi koṛa reaḱ katha

Sedae jǫkhẹn, kathae, miťṭań koṛa gạiye gupi kan tahẽkana; adǫ uni koṛa dǫ gupi gupitegeye hara juạnena.

Adǫ kathae, aghạṛ cando jǫkhẹn bir reaḱ kuṛiť rama jạnum dǫ ạdi bạrić bele akane ńẹlketa. Adǫ gạiko hõ ạdiko ạtiń kan khać dǫe mẹnketa, Noa kuṛiť rama jạnum beleń jǫmlege. Adǫ onka mẹnkate ona jhõṛ ṭhene calaoente jạnum beleye jǫjǫm kana.

---

9 See p. 47, note 5.

10 See above, note 7.

11 When bride and bridegroom arrive at the village of the bridegroom, a number of ceremonies are gone through, thus they are, here also, anointed and have to go from house to house to have their feet washed and to be fed with molasses.

12 When the official part of a ceremony is over, the guests are solemnly bidden farewell. They may often remain longer, but they are not any more guests for a special ceremony or feast. The formalities are over, and every one is at liberty to go away.

5 1 Santal children are set to work in the household, as soon they can be of use. Boys and girls are sent out to look after the cattle at a very early age. The 'education' they receive in this way is of a low order, and the cattle suffers just as much. It is rather out of the common that a boy continues as a cattleherd after he has grown to maturity; but, of course, it happens.

They let the dog lie on the young man's bedstead, and thus they were lying together for a long time. When it was night and all were asleep, they tell, the dog was in the habit of getting out of that dog's body and going out. The young man spied on her and found this out.

So one night he pretended to have fallen asleep. The girl then came out of her dog's body and was just starting to go out; at that moment the young man suddenly caught her in his arms and threw the dog's skin into the fire in the fire-place, so it was all burnt to ashes.

Now that dog became a human being, and they saw her; a human being and at the same time a spirit, such she was in appearance. Then all of them became very pleased and praised the young man very much.

Seeing the young man's wife, a boy companion of his said to himself: "Dash it[9], I will also marry a dog. This fellow married a dog and got such a beautiful wife. I shall do the same."

Really and truly this young man importuned his relatives to get a dog-wife, and they really arranged for such a one and settled the preliminaries and erected the marriage-shed. When they came to anointing the dog with oil and turmeric, she howled awfully, and at the time of *sindrạdan*[10] she did the same. Still in spite of all this howling they brought her along. But also when she came to their house, she howled in the same way, so they had to use force anointing them[11] with oil and turmeric. When they bade farewell to her male relatives[12], she started running all she could; she would not remain. "Look, look," they said to him, "see her over there, your wife is running off. Do make an end with her."

When he went to bring her back, she only howled something awful and commenced straight away to bite. So he let her off, the wretch. When he could not bring her back, they laughed mercilessly at him, and he felt such shame, that he did not say a word. And a couple of days afterwards the young man for very shame went and hanged himself.

That is the end of this story. It is thus much.

5. THE STORY OF A COWHERD

ONCE upon a time in the old days, they tell, a young man was herding cows; he had been doing this since he was a boy[1] and had grown to maturity herding cattle.

So it once happened in the month of aghāṛ[2], he saw a kite's talon thorn-bush[3] in the forest, full of ripe fruit. As the cows were occupied grazing, he said to himself that he would eat some of the fruit at once, and intent on this he went to the bush and started eating fruit.

---

[2] Aghāṛ is the month from the middle of November to the middle of December; it is the time when the heavy rice and much else ripens.

[3] The name as given is the literal translation of the Santali name for *Zizyphus oxyphylla*, EDGEW., a common scandent bush with strong thorns. The fruit is eaten.

Adọ kathae, ona jhọ̃ṇḍ ṭhenge husiť boṅga janumte ramkate dhiriteko tẹn akadea, ar sẹ uṇi koṛa dọ bae baḍae kana, noa dọ husiť boṅgako tẹn akadea mẹnte. Khange uni boṅgae mẹnkeťa, Mẹn ya phalna, mẹn yam lẹbẹť akadiṅa.

Khange kathae, uni koṛa dọ cọṭko sẹngeye kọyọk̓ baṛayeťa. Adọ ạdi ā̃tteye metade khan, kathaeye ọcọk̓ena. Adọ uni koṛae mẹnkeťa, Okor yaṅ ńẹl ńameťmea?

Adọ kathae, uni boṅgae mẹnkeťa, Ma noa dhiri khon uṭkạu oḍokkạṅme, adọṅ bhọrama; adọ nahā̃k̓ jọtọm ńẹl ńamlea ar jọtọkoak̓ rọṛge nahā̃k̓em bujhạutakoa, muć reak̓ rọṛ hō̃ nahā̃k̓em aṅjọm ṭhika.

Adọ uni koṛae mẹnkeťa, Sạri sẹ nasem mẹneťa? Pasẹm ẹṛẹyediṅ kan?

Adọe metadea, Baṅa, sạrigeṅ metam kana, ọhọṅ ẹṛẹmea; ma uṭkạukaṅme.

Adọ sạri ona dhiriye ṭhelao ọcọk̓keťa ar rampha jạnum hō̃ jọtọe hoṭọr ọcọk̓keťa. Khange kathae, uni boṅgae oḍokena; adọe metae kana, Ma bhọr hoṭaṅme, gạị bako thirok̓ kantiṅa.

Adọ kathae, luture ọnkedea, ar ceťko cọṅ mantar baṛakate mẽťā̃hā̃ sẹnteye ap̓kedea. Khange kathae, jọtọ boṅgae ńẹl ńamkeťkoa ar rọṛ hō̃e bujhạu ṭhikkeťtakoa. Adọ unreye metadea, Nẽk̓ẽ iṅ bhọraťmea, ạikạ ọkọe ṭhen hō̃ alom lạị baṛaea, am bạhu ṭhen hō̃ alom lạia. Ar judim lạikeťa mẹnkhan, ọhọm ńẹl ńamlekoa ar rọṛ hō̃ ọhọm aṅjọm daṛeletakoa. Ma inạgeṅ metam kana.

Adọ uni koṛa hō̃ gạị sẹne calaoena. Adọ sạri je kichu boṅga dọ jọtọgeye ńẹl ńameť-kogea, ar muć rọṛ hō̃, kathaeye aṅjọm ṭhikeťtakogea.

Adọ tin din badre cọṅ, kathae, miťṭaṅ koṛae bạiyena, ran ranteko bhagaoena, bangeye besok̓ kan. Adọ cekate cọṅ nui koṛa dọ onko oṛak̓ sẹngeye calaoen, adọe mẹnkeťa, Bhala uni ruạk̓ koṛaṅ ńẹllege. Adọ uni ruạk̓ koṛa ṭhene calaoen khane ńẹlkede dọ, miťṭaṅ boṅga koṛamre duṛup̓kate, kathae, hoṭọk̓e lin akadea. Khange uni koṛa dọ hape hapete aćak̓ kicrića pāk-keťtaea, adọ kathae, uni boṅga dọ ona kicrićte dale dalkedea sẹ, bogeteye dalkedea. Ọṇḍẹ khone laga ńirkede khan uni koṛa dọe phạriạ goťena.

Adọ un khon uni koṛa dọ ojhak̓e bahnayena; adọ kathae, ḍaṅgra jọmko ṭhen hō̃ boṅga-koko sẹnlen khan, bogeteye lagakoa. Adọ kathae, un khon uni koṛa dọ ạḍiko bọṭọraea.

---

4 See p. 48, note 6.

5 What is here rendered 'fellow' is in Santali a particle used in addressing boys and men younger than the speaker. It has a flavour of familiarity and sometimes of contempt.

6 All animals are supposed to be able to communicate with each other. In the folk-tales the talk of ants is rather commonly mentioned, just like here. The ants are seen everywhere, their industry, their way of working and their whole life will easily appeal to human intellect and cause wonder.

7 Possession by evil spirits is believed in by the Santals. The common idea is not that the spirit enters any-body; the general belief is that the spirit mounts a person, sits there and acts in some way, producing symp-toms of disease. The writer remembers once being told about a man, that a spirit jumped upon him when he was returning home from field-work. The spirit was so heavy that the man felt like a weight of two maunds, about 80 kilogr., on his back! He just managed to stumble along until he came to a tree near his home, when the spirit suddenly jumped off his back and up into the tree!

8 The Santals have two kinds of medicine-men, some who only give medicine, others who profess to find out the supernatural causes of disease and who, in addition to giving medicine, also do the 'necessary' to propitiate or drive away the evil spirits. These last ones are called *ojha*, a name derived from Sanskrit through Hindi. The boy here is, of course, understood to be an ojha, although his behaviour is rather out of the common way of ojha-procedure. See also p. 58, note 10.

Now here at this cluster people had blocked up with thorns a bonga, who had been expelled[4], and had put a stone on top; but the young man was, of course, ignorant of the fact that the stone was pressing down an expelled bonga. "Look out, young fellow," the bonga called out, "look out, young fellow, you so and so, you are trampling on me."

The young man was looking upwards; but when the bonga called out so loudly, he stepped aside and said: "Where are you, you fellow?[5] I don't see you."

"Please," the bonga said, "get me out and away from this stone; then I shall give you a blessing, and you will presently see us all and understand what all beings say; even the talk of the ants[6] you will be able to hear and understand."

"Do you speak the truth," the boy said, "or are you lying? Perhaps you are deceiving me?"

"No," he replied, "I tell you the truth, I shall certainly not deceive you. Please get me out."

So the young man really pushed the stone aside and with a stick also threw away the thorns which blocked the bonga up, all of them. The bonga then, they tell, came out. "Now please," the young man said to him, "be quick and give me your blessing; my cows won't be quiet."

Then, it is told, he blew into his ears and, having uttered some incantations, he made as if he washed his face. Thereupon the boy could see all bongas and also understand their talk. "There you see," the bonga said to him, "I have given you the blessing. Only be careful, don't tell this to anybody, don't tell it to your wife either. If you tell it, you will not any more be able to see them, and the ants' talk you will not be able to hear either. I tell you this."

The young man thereupon went towards the cows, and really and truly all the bongas who were there he could now see, and the talk of the ants he could also hear and understand.

Some time afterwards, they tell, a young man was seized with convulsions; they tried all kinds of medicines, but it was of no use; the boy did not in any way get better. Somehow or other the young man one day went towards the house of these people, saying to himself: "I should like to see that sick boy." When he came to the sick young man, he saw, look and behold, a bonga was sitting on his chest and throttling him[7]. The young man then quietly twisted his cloth into a rope and started beating the bonga with the cloth; he gave him a sound thrashing, and when he had driven the bonga away from there, the boy at once recovered.

From that time the young man was called a medicine-man[8]. Also when the bongas came to a place where they were eating oxen[9] he drove them all away, and from that time they were very much afraid of the young man.

---

9 The Santals do not like, often do not dare, to mention certain things or persons by their proper names. Here 'oxen' is used metaphorically for 'human beings'. It is a common belief with them that the bongas 'eat' people. How this 'eating' is done they are unable to explain. They agree that such 'eating' is the cause of many deaths. But while some suppose that the bongas eat the liver and lungs (as the witches are believed to do), and others are of opinion that the bongas want the blood and nothing else (giving as proof that at sacrifices people eat the flesh of most sacrificed animals, the bongas getting the blood only), many take the expression to be equivalent to destroying or to causing death. Some consequently think that the 'eating' is done before death, others take

Adọ kathae, uni koṛako bạhuadea, adọ uni bạhu hõe tahẽ rophayena.

Khange kathae, mit́ din dọ tikin jọkhẹn uni koṛa dọ duạr ṭhen dakae jọjọm kan tahẽkana; unre ọṇḍẹge muć dọ daka jọm lạgit́ko jarwayena. Unre kathae, barea muć ḍọ dakakin rẹpẹć kana arkin kạphạriạu kana. Adọ uni koṛa dọ arhõ dakae curućat́koa, adọ kathae, unkin dọ bẹbạrićkin jhogṛak' kana. Adọ unkin aṅjọmte uni koṛa dọ daka jọm hõe thirena, ar muluć mulućе landayet́ kana. Ar bạhuttẹt́ dọ tan mane ńẹṅẹl kana; adọ bae jivilet́a, hẹć sorkateye kulikedea, Cedak' bam jọmet́a ar cet́ onkam landayet́a? Enan khon in ńẹlet́mea, cet́ cọṅ muluć mulućem landayet́ kan. Adọ masẹ lạiaṅme, cetem landaket́a.

Adọ uni koṛae mẹnket́a, Okor baṅ cet́? Cet́ hõ baṅ landa akat́a.

Adọ ạḍiye jidket́a, menket́ae, Mage lạiaṅme, ar baṅkhan iṅ dọ baṅ tahẹna am ṭhen dọ. Am dọ ọkọe kuṛiko tuluć cọṅ menama; ona disạtem landayet́ kana.

Adọ uni koṛae mẹnket́a, Ona dọ baṅ kana, ẹṭagak' iṅ dọṅ landa akat́a.

Adọ uniye mẹnket́a, Ma ẹnte lạime. tọbẹ khan iṅ bataoa, ar baṅkhan ọhọṅ bataolea.

Adọ sạri bae bataolet khane lạiket́a, baṅma, Dakaṅ hirićlet́a, adọ ona ṭhen mućko jarwalena; adọ nonka onka bogeteko kạphạriạu kana; ona aṅjọmte iṅ dọṅ landa akat́a.

Adọ uni bạhuttẹte mẹnket́a, Cekate onkoak' rọṛ dọm aṅjọmket́a? Ale dọ okorle aṅjọmet́takoa.

Adọ unre uniye mẹnket́a, Baṅ, ọhọṅ lạilema. Mit́ hoṛe mẹn akawadiṅa, Ọkọe ṭhen hõ alom lạí baṛaea, am bạhu ṭhen hõ alo, ar baṅkhan ọhọm aṅjọmletakoa. Uni hoṛ onkae mẹn akawadiṅa, onateṅ metam kana, ọhọṅ lạilema mẹnte.

Adọ bạhuttẹte mẹnket́a, Ma lạime, ọhọ cekak'a, ar iṅ hõ ọhọṅ lạí baṛaea. Iṅ ṭhenge bam lạí khan, ọkọe ṭhenem lạia? Bam lạiaṅ khan, tọbe amren hoṛ dọṅ baṅ kana.

Adọ onka ạḍi lekae kiriạkede khane lạí dapoṛadea. Adọ kathae, ẹn hilok' khon dọ boṅga hõ bae ńẹl ńamkoa ar muć reak' rọṛ hõ bae aṅjọmtakoa.

Adọ ẹnẹ cabeyena katha dọ.

6. Mit́ṭaṅ boṅga ar Hoṛ koṛa reak' katha

Sedae jọkhẹn, kathae, mit́ṭaṅ koṛa gạiye gupi kan tahẽkana. Adọ tahẹn tahẹnte, kathae, Aghạṛ cando jọkhẹn bir sẹn gạiye idi akat́ko tahẽkana. Adọ gại ạcure sẹnlenre mit́ṭaṅ

it more literally, and think that they kill to feed on the dead body. What is here told is that, according to their belief, bongas may gather round a person dangerously ill to 'feed' on him, i. e. to cause his death. The 'hero' of the tale has received the gift of seeing the bongas, and makes use of his powers to chase the bongas away and consequently restore the patient to health.

10 Se p. 66, note 5. As a result of the way in which marriages are arranged with the Santals, it is always somewhat problematical whether the young people will hit it off or not with one another. When they do, it is often spoken of as here. It is always the girl who is supposed to have settled down and found her place in her new surroundings. Those who do not will generally run away.

11 A common suspicion here used as a weapon.

6 1 This story is, as will be seen, a variant of the preceding one. It is the same story told by some other people. It may be of interest to see, how it is varied. The story has many more details than the first one, all details giving a more coloured picture of Santal life and ideas. In the first story it was an expelled bonga which was set free. Here it is, strangely enough, the spirit of a dead man. The present-day Santals burn their dead ones, a custom which they tell they have adopted from the Hindus. They are, however, in certain cases buried, some for good, others only temporary. All children who have not been made full members of Santal society by

So they got a wife for the young man, and the girl also was content and stayed[10]. Now it happened one day at noon that the young man was sitting near the door, taking his food. Some ants came together there to eat rice, and two of them were trying to take rice from each other, and were bandying words; the young man then again gave them a little rice, and the two ants were quarrelling awfully. Listening to them the young man stopped eating and was smiling and laughing. His wife was staring at this, and when she could not restrain herself any longer, she went close to him and asked him: "Why don't you eat, and what are you laughing at in such a way? It is a long time I have been observing you, smiling and laughing at something. Do tell me, what is it you laughed at?"

"Why, nothing at all," the young man replied, "I have not been laughing at anything."

But she only persisted saying: "Do tell me, and if you will not, I shall not remain with you. You have certainly something to do with some girl or other[11]. You are thinking of that, therefore you are laughing."

"No, it is not that," the young man answered, "it is something else I am laughing at."

"Well then," she said, "tell it, so I shall give in to you; otherwise I shall never do that."

As she did not give in, he really told her and said: "I spilt some rice, and some ants came together at that, and quarrelled in such and such a way. It was hearing this that made me laugh."

"How is it," his wife asked, "that you could hear their talk? We other people, why, we do not hear what they talk."

"No," he answered, "I am not willing to tell that. Some one has said to me, 'Don't tell anybody, not your wife either, otherwise you will not be able to hear them.' That person has said so to me; therefore I tell you, I shall not let you know."

"Do tell me," his wife said, "it won't matter; I for my part shall, of course, not mention it. If you don't tell me, whom should you tell? If you don't tell it to me, I do not belong to you."

As she importuned and adjured him in this way, he finally told her. But from that day, they tell, neither did he see the bongas, nor could he hear the talk of the ants any more.

So the story is at an end.

6. A BONGA AND A SANTAL MAN[1]

ONCE upon a time in the old days, they tell, a young man was herding cows. So it happened that once in the month of aghāṛ[2] he had taken the cows towards the forest.

---

the caco chaṭiar ceremony being performed with them, are buried. Such become after death *bhuts*, which are supposed to be very small in size. People who die from cholera or smallpox are temporarily buried. When decomposition has set fully in — it does not take so long in an Indian climate —, the body is dug up and burnt. When a woman dies in childbirth or in pregnancy, the body is not burnt until the foetus has been removed. If such a woman remains buried, she becomes a curin, the same as the still-born child or the dead foetus. The curin is described as being very small and with a very large head. Both bhuts and curins are considered dangerous. The first ones harass and frighten people, taking on all kinds of shapes; the last ones are said to attack lonely people and suck their blood. All dead people are supposed to become bongas, except those who become bhuts and curins as described.

2 See p. 69, note 2.

dhũndre dọ kuṛiť rama bogete bele akane ńelkeť khan dọ ona jọjọme dhuṛauena. Gọṭeťae kọṭọkeťae, gọṭeťae kọṭọkeťae, ar rẹṭẹć rẹṭẹće jọmeť kana. Ar ona jạnum dhũnd phẹḍrege, kathae, tis jọkhẹn cọń hoṛko topaledea. Ona dọ bae hudiseť kana; ẹkẹn dhiriko dọhọ puńji akať mae ńẹleťge; mẹnkhan hoṛ topa dọ bae badeťa. Adọ ona dhiriko cetanrege dẹćkate ona kuṛiť rama bele dọe jọmeť kana. Ḍare ọr liveťeťa ar gọťkateye kọṭọkeť kana.

Adọ un jọkhẹn, kathae, onako dhiri bhitri khonge bońga dọ kathae roṛ gọťkeťa, Ẹya, Ẹya, mẹn ọcọkme, lẹbẹťediń kanam.

Khange uni koṛa dọ eṭak̓ sẹn roṛeť lekae ańjọmkeťte ona dhiri khon ãṛgoyente ona dhũnd latar sẹngeye oyoń baṛakeťa, adọ cele hõ bae ńẹl ńamleťkote arhõ ona dhiri cetanrege dẹćkateye jọmeť kana. Khange uni bońga dọ arhõ onkageye roṛ gọťkeťa. Khange uni koṛa dọe mẹneťa, Ayo, cele bae bheonayediń kan? Adọ ãṛgokate ọntẹ nọṭẹye bẹńgẹť baṛakeťa. Adọ cele hõ bae ńẹl ńamleťko khan, arhõ ọnḍẹge dẹćkateye jọjọm kana. Khange arhõ onkageye roṛ gọťkeťa, Ẹya, Ẹya, men ọcọk̓mem lẹbẹťediń kana.

Adọ unre uni koṛa dọe mẹnkeťa, Ọkọe ya, pe bọrọ ocoń kan? Okor iń ńẹl ńameťpea?

Adọ unre bońgae mẹnkeťa, Ma ọcọk̓me, nãhãk̓em ńẹl ńameńa.

Adọ sạriye ọcọk̓en khan, bońga dọ hoṛ lekae oḍokena. Adọe metae kana, ẹn kathae, Bam ńẹl ńameń kana?

Adọ uniye mẹnkeťa, Bań ńẹl ńameťmea. Ma adọ ceť lekateń ńẹl ńammea, ona lạiańme. Khangeye metadea, Ma sẹ ber ńẹleme, tin marań menaea.

Adọe ńẹlkede dọ, huḍiń tara siń ber menae. Adọe lạiadea, bańma, Ninạk̓ ber menaea.

Adọ ọntẹye bẹńgẹť ocokede jọkhẹnge, kathae, ceť cọe halań gọťkeťa. Adọe metae kana, Ma duṛup̓me. Adọe duṛup̓ ocokedea. Adọ, kathae, ceťte cọń mẽťe hoṭorkeťtaea; gantharge, kathaeye ọr toťkeťtaea. Khange kathaeye ńẹl ńamkedea. Khange adọe metadea, Mẹ̃ť mam saphakeťtiń; adọ lutur saphakatińme. Noko muć reak̓ roṛ bań ańjọmeťa, jẹmọn onkoak̓ roṛ iń ańjọmtako.

Adọ unreye metae kana, Hẽ, sapha mań saphaketamge, pasẹm lại? Judi jãhãe ṭhenem lạikeťa mẹnkhan dọ, ale hõ ọhọm ńẹl ńam daṛelelea, ar onko muć reak̓ roṛ hõ ọhọm ańjọm daṛelea.

Adọ uni koṛae mẹnkeťa, Ọhọń lại.

Arhõe metadea, Am bạhu ṭhen porjọntọ alom lại.

Adọe mẹnkeťa, Jọnọmre hõ ọhogeń lạilea.

---

[3] See p. 69, note 3.

[4] See above, note 1. When people are buried, it is generally only in a shallow grave, and stones etc. are put on the top to prevent jackals and other animals getting at the dead bodies.

[5] The Santals divide the time according to the position of the sun and, at night, of the moon and stars, and name the time in accordance with this or with work done or food taken at the particular time.

[6] The covering which prevents ordinary people from seeing those of the other world.

When he went to turn the cows back he saw that there was, in a thicket, a kite's talon bush[3] full of ripe fruit, and commenced to eat. He plucked and popped into his mouth, plucked and popped, and crunched and ate. Now close to that thorn thicket, they tell, a man had been buried some time ago[4]. He had no thought of this; he saw, of course, that stones had been piled up; but he had no idea that it was a grave. He was standing on the top of the stone heap and was eating the fruit. He was pulling down the branches, plucking and popping into his mouth.

While he was thus occupied, it is told, the bonga suddenly called out from the midst of the stones: "I say, you there! I say, look out, take yourself off! You are trampling on me."

The young man heard it like some one speaking from some other direction, and stepping down from the stones he peered into the thicket below the branches; but as he did not catch sight of anybody, he stepped up on the stones again and commenced eating. Then the bonga called out again in the same way. "O mother", the boy said, "some one is making fun of me." He came down again and looked round in all directions; but as he was not able to see anybody, he stepped up there again and continued eating. Then the voice called out again in the same way: "I say, you there! I say, look out, take yourself off! You are trampling on me."

Now the young man said: "Who are you, you fellows, who are frightening me?"

"Please, step aside," the bonga replied, "you will see me presently."

When the boy stepped aside, the bonga really and truly came out in the form of a human being, and spoke to him. "Don't you see me?" he said.

"No," the young man said, "I am unable to see you. Please tell me, how I shall manage to see you."

"Please look at the sun," the voice replied, "how high up is the sun?"

The young man looked and saw that the sun was about half way down[5], and said to him: "The sun is so and so high up."

While he made him look in that direction, the bonga picked up something or other and said to the boy: "Please sit down." When he had got him seated, he poked him in his eyes with something and pulled the covering film[6] away, whereupon the young man was able to see him. "My eyes," the man said, "you have certainly cleaned; clean my ears also. I cannot hear what the ants talk; please, that I may be able to hear their talk."

"Well," he replied, "I could certainly clean them for you; but perhaps you might let somebody know. If you told anybody, you would not any longer be able to see us, and you would not be able to hear the ants' talk either."

"I shall never tell," the boy said.

Again the bonga said: "Not even your wife must you tell."

"As long as I live," the young man replied, "I shall never tell."

Adọ onka ekraṛkate, kathae, luture ọṅkedea. Adọ khange, kathae, boṅgako hõe ńẹl ńamketkoa, ar muć reak galmarao hõe aṅjọm ṭhikkeṫteye bujhạukeṫtakegea. Adọ jähäre muć gẹlẹće ńamketa mẹnkhan, ọṇḍẹ dọ duṛupkateye aṅjọm mõṅjkoa, ar mulué mulućе landajoṅa. Ar boṅgako hõ jọtọye ńẹl ńamkogea. Ḍaṅgra jọm ṭhen hõ, kathae, hoṛ leka onkako sẹn jarwaka. Khange nui koṛa dọe ńẹlleko khan, bogeteye dalkoa are laga ńirkoa. Adọ onkae dal bhiṛkạuketko khan dọ nuiko ńelle khange, kathae, ọntẹ nọtẹ picọ pọcọko daṛjoṅa.

Khange onakate tin din badre cọṅ, kathae, aćren gate koṛa dọ ạdi bạrić rụa kạhilente mit din dọe bạiyena, nẹye gujuk lagadok kana. Adọ tikin jọkhẹn uni koṛa dọ gạiye aderkatketeye duṛup akan tahẽkana. Adọko lạiadea, baṅma, Amren gate koṛa dọe bại akana; baṅdọ nähäkko bes daṛeae baṅdọ baṅ.

Adọ ona katha uni koṛa dọe aṅjọmket khan dọe mẹnketa, Ọkọe tora ẹṇḍẹkhan iṅ ńẹl ạguyea. Adọ onka mẹnkateye calaoena.

Adọ racae bọlọyen khangeye họhọ sạḍeketa, Cele ho, menakpea sẹ baṅ? Ar aema hoṛ sẹn jarwa akante oṛakkore piṇḍạkoreko duṛup baṛa akana. Adọ uni gate koṛaren eṅgattẹt dọ nuiye ńẹlkede khan, rakate oṛak khone oḍokenteye metadea, Dela bạbu, nọtẹ bọlọkte gate koṛa ńẹletam.

Khange adọe bọlọyen khane ńẹlkede dọ, mitṭaṅ bhut koṛamreye duṛup akawadete họṭọke mocṛaoettae. Khange nui koṛa dọ ḍaṇḍare sili baber tahẽkantaea. Adọ onae raṛa gọtkette ona silitege uni bhut dọ carnaoe carnaokedea sẹ, bẹbạrićе carnaokedea. Khange bhut dọe kikiạu gọtketteye daṛet kana. Adọ gọṭa oṛakẹ lagakedete oṛak khon laga oḍokkedete duạr sẹnte goṭae carnao idikedete baṛge mucạt hạbićе carnao gọtkadea.

Khange uni gate koṛa dọe pharnaoenteye duṛupena. Adọ dakae khọjketkote dakako emadea. Adọ dakae jọmket khane bes utạrena. Adọ un khonko bạḍaekedea, nui hõe ojhakgea mẹnte.

Adọ onakate tin din badre cọṅ, kathae, mit din dọ oṛakre dọ ać bạhu eskargeye tahẽkana. Adọ ẹn hilok tikin jọkhẹn uni koṛa dọ gại aḍakatkote ać bạhuge dake taṅadete daka jọme ạbukente duạr ṭhenge daka jọme duṛupena. Adọ ọnḍẹge dakae aguadete bạhuttẹt do piṇḍạreye duṛupena. Adọ uni koṛa dọ dakae jọjọm kana, ar daka dọ mit bar sạkṛi hirić akana. Adọ ona jọm lạgit mõṛẽ turui gọṭẹn muć dọ ko jarwa akana. Ar onko muć dọ ona dakako rẹpẹć kana arko kạphạriạu kana. Adọ ona kạphạriạu aṅjọmte uni koṛa dọ daka jọm jọmkateye thirok kana, ar mọnẹ mọnẹte mulué mulućе landayet kana. Ar uni landayete ńẹlkede khan, bạhuttẹt dọe mẹnketa, Cet am mọtọm landayet kana?

---

[7] See p. 71, note 9. It is noteworthy that a human being is supposed to be able to chase away, not only one, but a crowd of spirits, when he can see them. It stands in absolute contrast to the very real fear which the Santals ordinarily have for the spirits. It is a common belief that disease may be caused by bongas who will 'eat', as it is called, that is, destroy human beings. What is here referred to is not the slaughtering and eating of bullocks. The expression is a figure. The 'bullock' means a human being, the 'eating' the disease supposed to be due to the inimical action of bongas.

[8] What is here described, is a very ordinary occurrence when somebody falls ill. Friends and relatives will come and sit watching, often crowds of them.

Having made the young man promise in this way, the bonga blew into his ears, and then, they tell, he could see the bongas and the talk of the ants he also could hear and understand. When he found traces of ants somewhere, he sat down there and enjoyed listening to them, smiling and laughing. The bongas he also saw, all of them. Where bullocks are being eaten, they also, it is told, come together, just like human beings[7]. When this young man saw them, he always gave them a good beating and drove them off. As he struck them in this way and frightened them away, the bongas, they tell, ran helter skelter away in all directions, as soon as they saw him.

After some time it happened that a boy companion of his became seriously ill, and one day he was seized with convulsions and was on the point of death. The young man had that day driven his cows into the cow-shed and was sitting down, when they came and told him: "Your friend has been seized with convulsions; it is uncertain whether they will be able to get him round or not."

When the young man heard this, he said: "Then I will at once go and see how he is," and saying this he went.

When he reached the courtyard, he called out: "Hallo there, are you here or not?" Now a large crowd of people had come together[8] and were sitting in the verandah[9]. As soon as the mother of his friend saw him, she came out of the house crying and said to him: "Come, my lad, come in here and have a look at your friend."

Having entered he saw him, and look and behold, a *bhut*[10] was sitting on his breast and twisting his neck. Now the young man had a hair rope round the loins; he untied this and commenced to lash the bhut with the hair rope; he gave him an awful lashing, so that the bhut screamed and ran away. He chased him round the house and out through the door, lashing him the whole way; he lashed him, until he drove him off at the end of the field on which the house was standing[11].

Thereupon his friend recovered and sat up and asked for food which they gave him, and when he had taken food, he became quite well again. From that time people recognized that this young man could also do the work of an *ojha*[12].

Some time, who knows how long afterwards it was, it happened one day that his wife was alone at home. At mid-day the young man had taken the cows to the resting-place[13]; his wife poured out water for him, and after having washed his hands he sat down at the door to take food. After having brought the rice to him there his wife sat down in the verandah[14]. As told, the young man was eating rice, and a few rice grains had fallen down from the plate to the ground. To eat these some five or six ants had come together, and these ants were fighting and quarrelling over the rice grains. Hearing this quarrel the young man again and again stopped eating and was smiling and laughing quietly by himself. When she saw him laugh, his wife said: "What are you laughing at alone by yourself?"

9–14 See pp. 78—79.

Adoe męnkeťa, Ceť hǫ baṅ.

Adǫ bąhuttęt dǫ ąḍi jid kukliye dhurąuena, kathae, Mage lạiaṅme. Daka utu baṅ jut iṅ ematmea, sę jutge, sę ceť lekam ṅęlkidiṅa onatem laṅdakeťa, sę ceť iạte?

Adoe męnkeťa, Daka utu hǫ besge, am hǫ besge.

Adoe męnkeťa, Tǫbę ceťem landakeťa? Ma lạime.

Adoe męnkeťa, Onaṅ landakeť katha dǫ lạlại baṅ ganoǩa.

Adoe męnkeťa, Ma lạime barę. Okoe ṭhen hǫ ohoṅ lại baṛaea.

Adoe metadea, Ohoṅ lạilema.

Khange bąhuttęte męnkeťa, Tǫbę amren hoṛ doṅ baṅ kana, tǫbęrege bam lạiaṅ kana. Am dǫ eṭaǩkom ṅamjoṅ kana, onage mǫnę mǫnętem landakeťa, ar onatege bam lạieťa.

Adoe męnkeťa, Ona dǫ baṅ kana. Am dǫ ạurige hona nhoam roṛeťa.

Adoe męnkeťa, Ente bam lạiaṅ kan khan. Ma tǫbę lạime, ar bam lại khan, iṅ dǫ ohoṅ tahẽlena. Ạpuṅ bareṅteko oṛakteṅ calaǩa.

Ar sęye męn akawadea, Okoe ṭhen hǫ alom lại baṛaea. Jăhăm lạikeťa męnkhan adǫ bam ṅęl ṅam daṛealea ar muć reaǩ rǫṛ hǫ adǫ ohǫm aṅjǫmletakoa. Ar bąhuttęt sę ąḍi jidą jide kukli kana. Adǫ ąḍiye jidkeť khan, kathaeye lại dapoṛadea. Adǫ kathae ęn hiloǩ khon dǫ boṅga bhut hǫ bae ṅęl ṅameťkoa, ar muć reaǩ katha hǫ bae aṅjǫmeťtakoa. En hiloǩ khon dǫ jǫtǫ maraoentaea.

Adǫ kathae, ona tayǫm dǫ ąḍi hoṛ ṭhen onka oṛe oṛe lạiaťkoa, baṅma, Nonka onkate nokoko doṅ ṅęl ṅameťko tahẽkana, ar noko muć reaǩ katha doṅ aṅjǫmeť tahẽkana. Adoṅ lạikeť khan jǫtǫ cabayena.

Ar katha hǫ jǫtǫ cabayena, in maraṅgea.

7. Boṅga aṅgęn

Sedae jǫkhęn, kathae, mitṭaṅ buru sendra gipitić phędre mitṭaṅ mare pukhri tahẽkana. Adǫ setaǩ jǫkhęn barea koṛa tirio oroṅ oroṅte ona pukhritege daǩ ṅũkin ăṛgolena. Khange boṅga kuṛi dǫ tamba sikṛite unkin koṛa dǫ jaṅgareye tǫl gǫťkeťkina. Khankin oḍoken khankin ṅęlkeťa, sutạm lekan sikṛiteye sikṛi akaťkin. Adǫkin or topaǩ gelaǩ kana, baṅge, kathae, topagoǩ kan; adǫ dhiritekin kǫṭęć topaǩeťa, adǫ ęnre hǫ, kathae, baṅ topagoǩ kan; adǫ orkin orkeťa sę, aemakin or jarwakeťa, ęnre hǫ baṅ mucạdoǩ kan. Arhǫkin thiroǩre ma hantę bhitritegeye or adereťkin kan. Khange bogetekin bǫtoroǩ kana.

---

9 Most Santal houses have a verandah. The walls of the house stand on a plint which extends a little outside the wall, just enough to let a man sit there on his haunches, on three sides, and somewhat more on the side where the entrance is. Here the eaves of the roof are lengthened so as to form a roof over the verandah which is here. The verandah is often fairly large and does service for a room.

10 See p. 70, note 7. — 11 See p. 52, note 15. — 12 See p. 70, note 8.

13 The cattle as a matter of course graze the whole year round; they are let out early in the morning and brought back in the evening at nightfall. In the middle of the day they are always taken to some place, generally near the village, where there are trees that give shadow; here they lie down to rest for a couple of hours.

"Nothing at all," he answered.

His wife then commenced to ask and kept persistently on. "Please tell me. Was the rice and curry I gave you not good; or was it good, or what did you see with me, since you laughed? What is it?"

"The rice and curry is nice," he said, "and you are nice too."

"Then what did you laugh at? Do tell," she continued.

"It would not do," he replied, "to tell what I laughed at."

"Do tell," she persisted, "I shall not tell it to anybody at all."

"I cannot tell you," he replied.

"Then I do not belong to you," his wife said, "that is why you do not tell me. You are seeking others[15]; that is what you laughed at by yourself, and therefore you will not tell."

"No, it is not that," he replied, "you are talking rubbish at random."

"Well," she said, "since you do not tell me. Therefore do tell me, and if you don't tell, I will certainly not stay with you. I shall go to my father and brothers."

Now the bonga had warned him: "Don't tell anybody. If you tell anybody, you will not be able to see us any more, nor will you be able to hear the talk of the ants further." On the other hand his wife persisted in asking him, and when she kept on in this way, he at last told her in disgust. From that day, they tell, neither did he see the bongas and the bhuts, nor did he hear the talk of the ants. From that day all was utterly lost to him.

Afterwards he told everything from beginning to end to a good many people. "In such and such a way," he said, "I was able to see those, and I also heard the talk of the ants. When I told others of it, it all came to an end."

And now the story is also all come to an end. It is thus much.

7. SPIRITED AWAY BY BONGAS.

ONCE upon a time in the old days it so happened that there was an old tank or pond near the place where the annual hunt spent the night[1]. In the early morning two young men went playing their flutes down to the pond to drink water. Down there a *bonga* girl suddenly bound the feet of those two young men with a copper chain. When they got out of the pond, they saw, look and behold, she had chained them with a chain like a thread. They pulled and tried to tear it to pieces, but it would not break. Then they tried to break it striking it with a stone; still it would not break. Then they tried to pull it out; they pulled and pulled and pulled out a heap of it; still the end would not come out. And when they stopped pulling, she was pulling the chain down into the water again, and the two boys became very much afraid.

14 The women first serve the men and eat, themselves, afterwards. It is of very seldom occurrence that a wife will sit down and take food at the same time as her husband.

15 A common expression about men who are tired of their wives and are arranging to get some one else.

71 Every year in the hot season — in the month of *baisak*, that is, from the middle of April to the middle of

Khange adọ bogete kạumạu kin họhọ keṭ khan, disom họṛko ńir calaoena; adọkin lạikeṭa, bańma, Onka nonkatẹ nọṇḍẹ dọliń hećlena, adọ nọ̃kọ̃eye sikṛi akatliña. Adọ noa sikṛi bańgeliń topak̉ daṛeak̉ kana, sojhe bhitritegẹye ọr adereṭliña; ar ọrte hõ bańge mucạdok̉ kana. Adọ dẹ, baba disom họṛ, chaḍaokaliñpe.

Khange disom họṛ ọrko ọrkeṭa sẹ, mimiṭ khạclạk̉ko ọr puñjiketa, ẹnre hõ bańge mucạdok̉ kan.

Khange kamarko ạguketkoa. Onko hõ kọṭẹć kọṭẹćteko lańgayena; bańge topagok̉ kan.

Adọ unkin koṛaren apatteko dihriko sap̉kedea, adọ uni hõ sunum boṅgakate boṅgae sap̉kedea, are manankeṭa; ẹnre hõ bae añjọmleṭa. Adọ dihriye mẹnkeṭa, Noa dọ, baba, iń họṭẹte ọhọ hoelena. Nukin koṛa dọ bae aṛak̉etkina, idikingeye mẹneṭa. Ma adọ apege je lekagepe budeṭ.

Adọ unkin koṛakin mẹnkeṭa, Ạliñren bhạyạdi menak̉pe khan, do oṛak̉te calak̉pe, ayo buḍhiạ ạguyepe. Jivẹṭre mẽṭ mẽṭliń ńẹpẹllenge; adọ ghuriạ̃ ọhọe ńelliña.

Adọ sạri bhạyạdiko calaoena oṛak̉te, ar disom phạd dọko uṭhạuena, ar unkin koṛaren peṛako dọ ẹnḍẹgeko tahẽyena. Adọ buḍhiạ họṛko ạguketkina, ar unkin sãote aema họṛko hẹć darayena; adọ bogetẹko rak̉ baṛaketa, ar unkin koṛa dọ dahe tabenko jọm ocoketkina, ar je kichu ạkinak̉ sapap̉ tahẽkana, jọṭọko ạgukattakina, adọkin ḍeṅga pherao baṛayena arko cọk̉atkina.

Adọ khange ona sikṛiteye ọr gọṭketkina, adọ jẹmọne ọreṭkina, tẹmọnkin calao idik̉ kana. Ar onko dọ ghuṭure teṅgokateko ńeńẹl kana, ḍanḍate, hatlak̉te, họṭọkte, adọkin unumena, ńẹl aṭketkinako. Adọ rak̉ baṛakateko ruạṛ hećena.

Adọ ọnẹ onka dak̉ren boṅga añgẹn reak̉ katha dọ. Ar adọm họṛ dọ dare ḍọḍh ọrre hõko añgẹn bọlọ akangea.

Adọ ẹnẹń purạuketa katha dọ.

May — the Santals have their large tribal hunts. All males who can go hunting. A man called *dihri* (possibly a Dravidian word, as *dihri* in Malto means a priest) is the leader, superintendent, priest and president of this hunt. He fixes date and place of meeting, performs the necessary sacrifices and presides at the nightly assembly, where all matters of public interest, specially concerning the people as such, as e. g. outcasting of Santals, are discussed and settled. Here all are as good as everybody else, a servant has the same rights as an overchief. This nightly council is their High Court, the Santals say. The people start on a Wednesday morning, hunt through a forest and meet in the evening at a place fixed by the *dihri*, called *gipitić*, that is, the place where they lie down, or pass the night together. Very few people sleep though. Many attend the sitting of the high council just mentioned. Especially the young people spend the night in all kinds of jollifications, drumming, playing the flute, singing and shouting. This part of the nightly doings may be, and generally is, on a low level. These hunt councils have in former days played a very important part in the tribal life of the Santals; like a good many other matters they are not any more what they used to be. The place of the *gipitić* is always chosen near some place where water is to be had.

2 When Santal individuals address an assembly sitting in council, they will frequently use the word *baba*, father, to show respect.

3 See p. 58, note 10. The *dihri* is the proper person to act at the hunt.

4 Vows are often made; a sacrifice or other specific performance is promised, to be given when what is asked for comes to pass.

The young men called out and made a great uproar and the whole hunt came running; they told their tale: "In such and such a way we two came here, and look, she has chained us both, and we are utterly unable to break this chain; she is pulling us straight into the water, and when we try to pull it out, there is no end to the chain. Please, honoured country-men[2], do deliver us."

The collected hunters thereupon pulled and pulled they each pulled a whole basket full; still there was no end to the chain.

Then they brought blacksmiths, and they hammered and beat, until they were tired; the chain would not break.

The fathers of the two boys then got hold of the hunt priest; he consulted the oil-oracle[3] and caught the bonga. He made a vow[4]; still she would not listen, and the hunt priest said: "This cannot, sirs, be solved through me. She does not set these two boys free; she intends to take them away. Please, therefore, you yourselves do whatever you think."

The two boys then said: "If any brothers[5] of ours are here, do go home and bring our mothers. We wish to meet them once more while we are alive; they will not see us any more."

Their brothers then went home, and the army of hunters also left; but the relatives of the two boys remained there. The two mothers were brought, and together with these two a large number of people came. They wept bitterly; so they gave the two boys *curds*[6] and *taben*[7] to eat, and whatever belonged to those two of implements and tools[8], they brought it all; so the two boys put on fresh loin clothes, and they kissed them.

Thereupon the bonga suddenly started pulling them with the chain, and as she was pulling, they went along. Standing on the bank others were looking on; they went down to the loins, up to the armpit, to the neck, then they were submerged. They saw them disappear. Then, having cried bitterly[9], they came back home.

Such is the story of people being spirited away by water bongas. Some people have also been spirited away and taken into hollow trees.

Now there I have finished that tale.

---

5 Cousins, second cousins, &c., are also styled brothers.

6 Curds, the same as kephir, commonly used among the Santals.

7 See p. 54, note 4.

8 It is customary at cremation to let all kinds of things accompany the dead one. These goods are put with the body on the bedstead, when it is carried away. Before fire is put to the funeral pyre, the things are all taken away and sold at a kind of auction immediately after the cremation, the money thus realized being spent to buy food or rice-beer for those who have assisted at the cremation. The goods are supposed to be of use in the other world. What is here related evidently refers to the custom mentioned, only that the two young men here take their implements with themselves directly.

9 The women at the time of death and afterwards occasionally start lamentations, always using a fixed kind of melody, varying the words according to need and circumstances. The men do not wail in this way, but often give way to inarticulate and bitter crying.

8. Boṅga tuluć bapla akan hoṛ reaṅ

Noa boṅga bapla, kathae, sedae do̱ ạdi canke tahe̱kana, ar boṅga ho̱ hoṛ ieka so̱do̱rko dãṛã baṛae kan tahe̱kana, ar hoṛ tuluć ho̱ko galmarao kan tahe̱kangea. Ar nitkate do̱ thoṛa etaṅ ṅo̱k̓ akana, onka so̱do̱r do̱ bako galmarao kana. He̱, ạdi so̱ndhe̱ mit̓ bar hoṛ tulućge. Ar noa reak̓ kạhnite̱t̓ do̱ pe̱ pon go̱ṭe̱n gan do̱ṅ baḍaea. Ona ho̱ ạiką hoṛ lạiak̓ kathage, sạri baṅdo̱ nase, onka ho̱ṛko lạiet̓a. Acha, ado̱ miṭṭaṅ ne̱tarkin bapla akan ar uni ho̱ṛṭe̱t̓ ho̱ jive̱t̓ge menaea, ona reak̓ kathage lahate do̱ṅ lại pạhilet̓a. Ona do̱ nonka kana.

Nią Jamkando̱r atorege Ramaeyić miṭṭaṅ koṛa menaea, ar Pạdum do̱e hijuk̓ se̱nok̓ kante jạnice baḍaegea; ar uni koṛa ho̱ paset̓e ṅe̱l akadege co̱ṅ cet̓ co̱ṅ. Ado̱ uni reak̓ katha do̱ nonka kana. Ona Jamkando̱r pạchim nakhare gạḍa so̱ḍo̱k̓ phe̱dre miṭṭaṅ dhiri huṭup̓ menak̓a. Ona do̱ jaṅge dhiriko ṅutum akat̓a; o̱ne̱ Pạdume ṅam akat̓ sokṛa latar munucạt̓ ṭhenge menak̓a.

Ado̱ kathae, ona dhiri ṭhen do̱ kuṛi boṅga menaea. Sedae onakore bir tahe̱kan jo̱khe̱n do̱, kathae, gidrą kuṛi leka ona dhirikoreye duṛup̓ baṛaea. Ar oka hilok̓ oka hilok̓ do̱, kathae, ho̱ṛe ṅe̱lleko khan do̱ thạrire daka ar bạṭire jel utu sajaokateye o̱ḍokkak̓ kan tahe̱kana. Ado̱ jãhãege he̱re̱l ho̱po̱n o̱nṭe̱ko se̱nlen khan do̱e metakoa, Ne̱, peṛa, daka jo̱mkatiṅpe, ạḍi jut iṅ daka utu akat̓a. Ne̱ se̱ e̱nte, jo̱m gelak̓tiṅ me, cet̓ leka bhalaṅ isin aro akat̓a. Onka kathaeye metako kan tahe̱kana. Ado̱ kathae, bo̱to̱rte cele ho̱ daka jo̱m bako re̱be̱na; ar uni do̱ onka ạdi ạjijkateye metakoa, e̱nre ho̱ bako jo̱mtaea.

Ar kathae, ona jo̱khe̱n do̱ atore jãhãe ṭhen bapla bihą kamko oramle khan, ar thạri bạṭitem o̱kulanok̓ khan do̱, kathae, ạyup̓ jo̱khe̱nem calaoena arem me̱n o̱ṭokat̓a, Gapanok̓ iṅ ṭhen peṛako hijuk̓ kana; thạri bạṭiteṅ o̱kulanok̓ kana; emaṅme, gapaṅ iditama. Enka ro̱ṛ o̱ṭokate, kathae, e̱n hilok̓ do̱m ruạṛ he̱ćena. Ado̱ dosar hilok̓, kathae, am do̱ bhạrią khạclạk̓ ante setak̓ jo̱khe̱n khạtirjoma calao go̱dok̓me, ado̱ kathae, ona dhiri cạṭạnire gạḍa gu̱ḍ o̱ḍok jarwa akat̓em ṅam go̱da, ado̱ cure mar khạclạk̓rem bhoraoket̓a. Ado̱ tin dinem do̱ho̱ea, iną katham ro̱ṛ o̱ṭokat̓a, ado̱m ạguket̓ge. Ar idikak̓ hilok̓ do̱, kathae, jo̱to̱ge ṅe̱l ṅe̱ltem maṅjao saphaket̓a, je̱mo̱n sạkṛi do̱ oka ṭhen ho̱ alo tahe̱n. Ado̱ onka ạrik pạrik gitil maṅjaokate ạyup̓ jo̱khe̱n arho̱ ona dhiri cạṭạniregem idikat̓taea, arem ro̱ṛ o̱ṭokat̓a, Thạri bạṭiṅ idilet̓tama, ado̱ no̱k̓o̱e iṅ ạgukat̓tama; ma baetam. Ado̱ enka me̱n o̱ṭokate ado̱ko ruạṛ he̱ćenge. Ado̱ kathae, o̱ne̱ onka sedae do̱e e̱mok̓ kan tahe̱kana.

---

[1] The bunch of stories given under this heading are, as will be seen, not folk-tales in the ordinary meaning of the word. They have, however, been included here for several reasons. They give an excellent insight into the Santal mind and way of thinking and partly living; they show how strong a hold superstition has on them; they may possibly give an indication of how stories of the kind here told have originated, both how they may be due to superstitious misunderstandings, and how they have been adapted by the local story-tellers. The last of the three tales is so intensely realistic and at its close pathologically so correct, that one cannot avoid thinking that some real happenings are related.

It might be mentioned that the Santal who has written this down is an otherwise sensible man, a bit of a philosopher with a tendency to "preaching". The stories here related are written down, because he was especially requested to tell what he knew. Most Santals have some belief in the possibility of such happenings as those related, perhaps not quite so much in evidence now as was the case formerly.

8. TALES OF SANTALS WHO HAVE MARRIED BONGAS[1]

To be married to a *bonga* was formerly, it is told, of frequent occurrence; then the bongas were also walking about openly like human beings; they were also talking with people. Now at the present time this has become somewhat seldom; they do not thus openly enter into conversation with people, well, very sparingly with one or two. I know some three or four stories about this matter; only remember, they are stories which people tell; whether they are true or not, people tell them so. Well then, there is a man who has been married (he is still living), about whom I am first going to tell. It is as follows.

In the village of Jamkandor lives a young man named Ram. Padum[2] constantly visits that village, so he is likely to know of it; he has perhaps also seen this young man. His story is as follows. In the neighbourhood of Jamkandor to the west near a river bed there is a rock, which they call the bar-stone. It is at the lower end of the *sokra*[3] that Padum has acquired.

At that rock, they tell, there is a bonga girl. Formerly when there was forest in those parts, they tell, she was in the habit of sitting on those stones in the shape of a small girl. Now and then, they tell, when she saw people, she was in the habit of putting rice on a brass plate and meat-curry in a brass bowl and setting this out, and when any man came that way, she said to them: "Please, my friend, partake of my rice; I have prepared some very nice meat-curry. Do please then, just taste and feel how I have prepared food". In this way, they tell, she spoke to them; but they were afraid, and no one would eat her rice. In spite of her beseeching them in this manner they did not take her food.

It is further told that if people at that time had commenced to make the necessary preparations for a marriage in the village, and they ran short of brass plates and cups, then you might go there in the evening and say: "To-morrow guests are coming to me; I have not enough brass plates and cups; lend me some, I shall take them away to-morrow." After having said this you came away that day; the next morning you might confidently go with shoulder-stick and baskets, and you would find heaps put out on that rock, and you might fill your baskets as quickly as you liked. Then you just stated how many days you would keep the goods, and so you came away. The day you took it all back, you had to look very carefully and scour and clean them all, in order that no leavings of food[4] should remain anywhere. Having scoured them all with sand and made them spotlessly clean you took her goods and put them back again on that rock in the evening and said, as you did so: "I took your brass plates and cups away, and here I have now brought them back again. Put your things safely away." Having spoken in this manner you came away. In this way, they tell, she was in the habit of lending formerly.

---

[2] Padum to whom is referred as a witness was for more than twenty years in the service of the present writer, up to his death some years ago. The village Jamkandor is some eight miles away from the writer's home in India. Padum's land was in this village.

[3] [4] See p. 84.

Adọ kathae, ọkọe cọn mit́ dhao dọe ạgulet́ tahẽkan. Adọ idikak̓ jọkhẹn bes dọ bako mańjao saphalet́a, okakore cọn sạkṛige tahẽyen. Adọ kathae, un khon ona thạri bạṭiko dọ bae ẹmok̓ kana. Ar inạk̓tege bir hõ ṭạṇḍiyena, jọtọ poṭor cabayena.

Adọ kathae, nãhãk̓kate uni Ramaeyić koṛa dọ cekakote cọe bulạu oco akan, bańdọ uniak̓ daka utugeye jọmket́tae, bańdọ cet́teye bulạu akan, onako dọ bań kuli baṛa akadete bań baḍae akana. Ar uni koṛa hõ menaegea, calao hijuk̓ kangeae. Dinre bar belakateye calak̓ kana, tikin jọkhẹn mit́ dhao dọ, ar mit́ dhao dọ ạyup̓ jọkhẹn.

Ar kathae, oka hilok̓ dọ uni boṅga kuṛige mạńjhi hopọnera chinteye hijuk̓ kana, adọ notẹ khon mit́tege calak̓ko ńẹlkina. Adọ ona dhirikokin tiok̓le khangem ńẹl adea. Ar ọnḍẹ sẹṭẹrkatem sẹnlen khan arem mẹnle khan, Bhala cet́kin cekayet́a, sẹ cet́kin galmarao kana? Delabo ańjọm ạgukina; adọm sẹnlen khan, hoṛtẹt́ dọ bam ńẹl ńamea, mẹnkhan roṛ reak̓ aṛańṭẹt́ dọm ańjọmgea. Adọ pusṭạu bań ańjọm ṭhikok̓a. Arem mẹnle khan, Bhalań tãṛãk̓-kok̓a; oka ṭhen khone bọlọk̓ kana ńẹleań, adọ ḍher hoṛ onkako tãṛãk̓ gela akana; adọ bańgeko ńẹl bọlọ daṛeaea. Ńẹleako mẹnte tikin jọkhẹn hõ, kathae, ḍher hoṛko tãṛãk̓a, arko mẹnkak̓a, Jọtọ hoṛtebon tunkhiyea, bhala oka ṭhen khone bọlọk̓ kana mẹnte. Adọ kathae, hoṛko tahẹnre hõ nui koṛa dọe calao gọdok̓gea; adọ ṭheṅga ar tirio dọ ghuṭureye dọhọ gọt́kat́ge; adọ hako capo mẹnte gaḍa sẹne ãrgo gọdok̓a. Adọ hinạ bhuk̓ hõe soga, nhiạ bhuk̓ hõe soga, adọ enka enkategeko ńẹl at́kedege. Adọ sẹn sorok̓teko ńẹlea arko mẹna, Henda ya, nẹnḍẹgebo ńẹlledea, adọ bhalae oka gọt́ena? Adọko ńẹl at́kedea, bako ńam daṛeadea. Ar roṛ ma bhitrire gandar gundurko ańjọmet́ge. Adọ bar ghonṭa gan amdaj ọnḍẹye tahẽyenge, arhõe oḍok hẹćenge. Adọ nitre hõ onkako ńẹl akadea, adọ kuli thọ ọkọe hõ bako kuli akadea, ẹkẹnko ńẹl hape akadegea.

Adọ ọnẹ onka niạ Jamkandọrre dọ ńẹlak̓ kathako lạiet́a. Kạhni dọ bań kana. Ar uni koṛa dọ nit hõ menaegea, ar jaoge onkae calak̓ kangea. Adọ niạṭak̓ katha dọń cabaket́a.

Arhõ onka boṅga tulućko bapla akan hoṛ reak̓ kathage. Ar ńẹlak̓ katha kangea, ar uni hoṛ hõ nit hạbić menaegea. Uni hoṛ dọ hana Pạṛ disomre Kusbạ hạṭ khon pạchim sẹn buru kocare Kesaphuli ato menak̓a. Ona atore goṅgońteko menak̓koa. Ar uni goṅgoń hopọn koṛa dọko pẹ boehak̓a, ar kuṛi dọkin bar hoṛgea; jọtọre mõṛẽ boehawako. Adọ uni huḍiń koṛa dọ kạḍa bitkile gupi kan tahẽkanre dọ tirio bẹbạṛiće ọrọńẹt́ tahẽkana. Ar uni koṛa dọ Sunạwaea.

---

3 Sokṛa is the name given by Santals to a low area or depression in sloping ground, in which rice-fields have generally been prepared. It is too small to be called a valley.

4 Elsewhere these "people" are described as taking human food. It seems to be leavings that she detests.

5 The whole story may have its explanation here.

6 At certain times of the year it is not uncommon for people to catch fish and crabs in the manner described. There is very little water, and the fish etc. may be found in small cavities in the bank and are easily caught with the hands.

7 A characteristic trait with the Santals; they do not like to tackle a delicate matter directly, and may do as here described.

8 The flute is the most common musical instrument with the Santals, and there are few boys that cannot play it. The ordinary flute is made from bamboo, with seven holes, one of these for blowing. Especially young men who

Then it once happened, they tell, that somebody had borrowed from her, and when he brought them back again, they had not scoured and cleaned the things properly; here and there a few leavings of food remained. From that time, they tell, she does not give these brass plates and cups any more. By that time the forest had also been cut down; the whole country had become denuded of trees and bare.

But at the present time, they tell, the young man Ram has somehow or other — who can tell how — been seduced, whether it has happened through his eating her rice and curry, or it has been through some other means, — he has not been asked about this, so it is not known. The young man is living; he goes and comes. He goes to the place twice daily, once at noon, and again once in the evening.

They further tell that this bonga girl now and then comes in the likeness of the daughter of the village headman[5]. People see them from near the village walking together; but when they reach that rock, he disappears out of sight. And if you go right up there and say by yourself: "What are they doing?" or: "What are they talking together?" — then you will not be able to see anybody; but you may hear the sound of voices, although it cannot be heard distinctly. If you say you will watch and see from where he enters, then many people have tried to lie in wait in this way; but they have been utterly unable to see him enter the rock. In order to see him, they tell, many people go to watch also at noon time, and say: "We shall, all of us, keep him in sight and find out from where he enters the rock." But even if the people remain there, the young man goes straight on, puts his stick and flute on the river bank and then goes down to the river to catch fish with his hands[6]. He puts his hand into one hole, and then into another, and in this way they lose sight of him. Then they go near to the place and look for him and say to each other: "I say, how is this? Here on this spot we saw him; what in the world became of him?" They lose sight of him and are not able to find him, while they hear someone speaking inside in low tones. The boy then remains for about two hours, whereupon he again comes out. Quite recently they have also seen him in this way; still they have not put any questions to him, they have only seen him and kept quiet[7].

Such is what they have seen in Jamkandor, which I have here told. It is not a fairy-story. This boy lives at the present day, and he is constantly going and coming in this way. Now I have finished this story.

Here is another story of a man who has been married to a bonga girl. This is also something which has been seen, and the man concerned is also still living. This man lives in the Pạṛ country to the west of Kusbạ-haṭ up against the hills in the village of Kesaphuli. The family of my father's elder brother lives in this village. This uncle of mine has three sons; he has two daughters. They are in all five brothers and sisters. The youngest son was in the habit of constantly playing the flute[8], while he was herding the buffaloes. The name of this young man is Suna.

Khange ńel̤me se̤, mitṭań ul jharnaren kuṛi boṅga do̤e bulauente uni koṛareye laṭkaoena. Khange mit́ din do̤ kaḍa bitkilkoe gasao baṛaket́kote tara siṅ ber do̤ ona ul jharna se̤ngeye mohṇḍa go̤t́kat́koa. Ar un jo̤khe̤n do̤ Bai̤sa̤k cando tahẽkana. Khange kaḍa bitkil do̤ko lahayena, ać do̤ um baṛakt́egeye tayo̤mena. Ado̤ tirio̤ o̤ṛoṅ o̤ṛoṅte tayo̤m tayo̤mteye pańja idiyet́koa. Ar ona jharna cetan ṭhen do̤ mit́ go̤ṭe̤n marań utar dhiri caṭani menak̕a. Ado̤ ona caṭani cetanrege uni boṅga kuṛi do̤e duṛup̕ akana.

Ado̤ uni koṛae se̤n se̤ṭe̤ren khan do̤e ńe̤le kana, ṭhik ṭhak aćren talayić hilittet́ lekage. Ado̤e ńe̤lkede khan do̤e me̤nket́a, Ayo! teheń do̤ ać eskar cet́ lagat́ no̤ṇḍe̤ do̤ he̤ćkateye duṛup̕ akana, se̤ bhala dadań hõ menaea? Ado̤e be̤ṅge̤t baṛaket́ do̤, celege ba̤nuk̕ko. Khange ado̤e me̤nket́a, O̤ko̤e tora bhala se̤nkateń kuliyea ać eskargeae, se̤ o̤ko̤e tuluće he̤ć akana, se̤ usa̤t́geye he̤ć akana. Se̤nkateń kulilege. Ado̤ onka me̤nkate uni ṭhene se̤n sorenteye kulikedea, Henda hili, cedak̕ am eskar no̤ṇḍe̤ do̤m duṛup̕ akana? Ukurić dadań do̤?

Ado̤ uniye me̤nket́a, Hẽ, dadam do̤ ba̤nugića; iń eskargeń he̤ć akana.

Ado̤e metadea, Cedak̕em he̤ć akana?

Ado̤ uniye me̤nket́a, Am tulućge mitṭań galmarao menak̕a, onateń he̤ć akana ar iń pańja akat́mea.

Ado̤e metadea, Cet́ galmarao? Din hilok̕ co̤ṅ mit́ ṭhenge menak̕bon, ar a̤yup̕ do̤ ba̤ń calak̕te noa bir pakaṛ do̤m sendrayedin kana? Cet́ lekan katha kana, ma la̤ime. Iń do̤ń hudisket́a, pase̤t́ usa̤t́geye he̤ć akan co̤ṅ cet́ co̤ṅ. Ado̤ o̤ne̤m me̤net́, mitṭań katha badatteń panja akat́mea; ado̤ ma se̤ la̤i ho̤dme, cet́ lekan katha kana.

Ado̤ uniye me̤nket́a, Katha do̤ a̤ḍi jut katha kana. Ado̤ nãhãk̕em khusia̤tiń baṅdo̤ baṅ, bejãe te̤rge̤ń macha lekam ro̤ṛet́a. Baṅdo̤ń la̤iamre ganok̕ ba̤ṅdo̤ bań la̤i. Am ṭhen la̤ia me̤nte noa birre sendra ńamket́meteń he̤ć akana, ado̤ am hona eṭak̕gem metań kana. Ado̤ ińak̕ katham do̤ho̤e khan iń ro̤ṛa, ar bam do̤ho̤e khan do̤ ba̤ń ro̤ṛa.

Ado̤ uni koṛae me̤nket́a, Ma cet́ katha kana hare phare ro̤ṛ ho̤dme. Idi o̤ṭo kamań. Mań hẽket́a, ro̤ṛme, ańjo̤mgetamań. Ar se̤ ṭhik aṛań hõ uniak̕ aṛań lekageye ańjo̤mket́a.

Ado̤ unreye me̤nket́a, Ia̤ hudińić, katha do̤ noa kana: teheń do̤ am tuluć ro̤ṛ landae lagat́ mo̤n calao akantińa. Me̤nket́ań, okare bań nui do̤ń ńame? Ado̤ onate am ńam ńamtege noa bir pakaṛ do̤ń sendra a̤gu akat́mea.

Ado̤ uni koṛae me̤nket́a, Hẽ ma hẽge, hili; pase̤ dadańe baḍaelań, bae edrealańa?

Ado̤ uniye me̤nket́a, Cekate bań uni do̤e baḍae? Ńel ṭhikok̕ak̕ se̤ye oroma. Cekateye baḍaea? Ado̤ amgem la̤i baṛae khangeye baḍaelańa. Iń do̤ jo̤no̤mre hõ o̤ho̤geń la̤ilea.

---

are out herding buffaloes at night, may be heard playing the flute incessantly. They enjoy it and likely think others do the same.

9 The well-known mango tree, *Mangifera indica, L.*, generally planted.

10 See p. 79, note 1.

11 *Hili* is the wife of an elder brother; the relationship between her and the younger brothers of her husband is what is called landa sagai, see p. 63, note 7. They are generally on very intimate terms. A kind of polyandry may be found here. If a *hili* should live with a younger brother of her husband, no one seems to say anything, provided the husband will allow it.

Now then listen, a bonga girl living in a spring at a mango[9] tree fell in love with that young man and clung to him. It happened one day that he, after having scrubbed the buffaloes and buffalo cows, in the early afternoon drove them towards that mango spring. It was in the month of bạisạk[10]. The buffaloes got in front of him, he himself fell behind bathing, and, playing the flute as he went along, he followed after them in their tracks. Now, just above the spring mentioned there is a very large rock, and on that rock this bonga girl was sitting.

When the boy reached the place, he saw her, exactly like the wife of his second oldest brother. When he caught sight of her, he said: "O mother, for which purpose has she come here alone to-day and is sitting there? or perhaps my elder brother is here also?" But when he looked round, no one was to be seen. He then said: "I shall go at once and ask her whether she is alone, or with whom she has come, or perhaps she has come because she sulks. I shall go and ask her first of all." Having this in mind he went up to her and asked her: "I say, *hili*[11], why are you sitting here alone? Where is my brother?"

"Well," she replied, "your brother is not here; I have come alone."

"Why have you come?" he asked her.

"I have a matter to talk with you about," she replied, "therefore I have come and followed you here."

"What kind of talk?" he asked; "why, we are every day together in one place, and as I do not go anywhere in the evening, why do you hunt me up here in the jungle? What kind of matter is it? Let me hear. I thought that you had perhaps come sulking. Now you say that you have followed me on account of something; tell then at once what kind of a matter it is."

"Oh, it is a very nice matter," she replied; "the question is whether you will be pleased with what I have to say or not; you are so nagging in your way of speaking. Who knows whether it will do for me to tell you, or perhaps I should not tell. I have come and hunted you up in this forest in order to tell you, and then you are saying that other thing to me. If you will listen to me, I shall speak; if you will not, I shall not."

"Well," the young man said, "what is it? say it quickly. I shall see you back home. I agree; please speak; I shall listen to you." Now her voice was also exactly like the voice of the other girl.

"I say, small one," she replied, "it is this: to-day my mind has gone out to talk and laugh with you. I said to myself: wherever shall I be able to meet him? That is why I have hunted you up here in the jungle."

"Quite so, *hili*," the young man said; "but perhaps my brother will find us out, will he not then be angry with us?"

"How should he know?" she replied; "he will only recognize what can be seen. How should he be able to know? Well, if you will tell, then, of course, he will know. I for my part shall never tell at all."

Adǫ uniye mǫnkeťa, Dal ocoḱ lagať iń ḷaia? Iń ki bǫtǫr bạnuḱtińa?

Adǫ uniye mǫnkeťa, Ǫtę cǫń, ęnḍękhan jǫtǫ kathalań gulạnḍkeťa. Ma tǫbęlań hako pakoea. Adǫ ęnękin kaj baṛakeťa.

Adǫ khange mǫn dǫ cekayentạkin cǫń, miť ṭhen khon alo chapaḍaoḱge sanayeťkina. Adǫ ceťko cǫkin galmarao kan, menaḱkinge. Ar kaḍa bitkil hǭ inạkorege palakoko jǫjǫm kan, menaḱkoge. Ar nukin hǭ khilḍu khamḍa kan menaḱkinge, oṛaḱte kole hǫe hiṛińkeťa; ńuhum hạbić menaḱkinge. Adǫ uni koṛawaḱ mǫn cekakote cǫń ạcurentae, disạkeťe ńuhumen. Adǫe metadea, Durrǫ! bam sǫnlena. Nit dǫ ǫkǫe tulućem calaḱa? Delań miťtege; noko hǭlań laga torakoa. Ar nãhãḱ dhorage teheń dǫ oṛaḱreko ńam baṛayeťme kana, ar nãhãḱ dadań dǫe dal gǫć utạrlańa.

Adǫ uniye mǫnkeťa, Ǫhǫe dallańa. Uni dǫ miť ghạriteń ęrę gǫdea.

Adǫ enka mǫnkate ęnękin laga ạguyeťkoa. Adǫ inạ kulhi mucạťre khangeye metadea, Iạ huḍińić, ma am dǫ lạga ạgukom, iń dǫń lahaḱ kantalańa. Bhalań ańjǫmkoa, ceťkoko edren kana mǫnte. Miťte dǫ balań sęṭęroḱa.

Adǫe metadea, Ma tǫbę khan lahaḱme. Adǫ enka mǫnkate uni dǫe kol lahakedea. Adǫ ęnḍę khone pharakena, adǫe okayen cǫń. Ar uni koṛa dǫ bae baḍaeleťa, nui dǫe bońga kuṛi kana mǫnte dǫ.

Adǫ ạditęť uni bońga kuṛi dǫe pạrkạuena. Jaoge uni hilit chintekin ńapama, ar oka dǫ oṛaḱ khon hǫe bereť idiyea, adǫ ęnrehǭ bańgeye pǫhǫm daṛeae kana. Adǫ bǫchǫr din lekakin tahęyena.

Khange miť din dǫ tala ńindạ jǫkhǫn oṛaḱ khone bereť oḍokkedea. Adǫ kathae, baṛge duạr ṭhenge oḍokoḱ lekae disạleťa, adǫ cekae bhul gǫťkede cǫń. Adǫ ńęlme sę, oka okate cǫe idi gǫťkedete ona ul jharna cetan dhiri cạṭạnire sǫnkatekin duṛuṕ akan arkin mǫ̃ńjjoń kan.

Ado tin ǫktęre cǫń, kathae, uni koṛawaḱ disạ dǫ ạcurentaete ona ul dareko jharna sǫḍǫḱko ar cạṭạnikoe beńgeť baṛawať khane mǫnkeťa, Durrǫ! noa tala ńindạ okareye ạgu akadińa? Nui hilińdǫ ṭhik hǫṛ dǫe bań kana. Nui dǫe oka lekan hǫṛ kan cǫń. Nonka uni koṛa dǫ ać mǫnę mǫnęteye hudiskeťa.

Adǫ arhǭ, kathae, miť ghạri khange tinre cǫń oṛaḱrekin hęć gǫten. Adǫ arhǭ mit ębhęn gitićkate ena sim dǫko raḱkeťa. Ar uni dǫe okayen cǫń, ać eskargeye gitić akan. Ar ona katha uni koṛa dǫ mǫnre tahęyentaea. Adǫ setaḱ baskeaḱ ber khange uni koṛa dǫ hilitťęte kulikedea. Metae kanae, Henda hili, teheń ńindạ dǫ okatem idilidińa?

---

[12] The Santals generally have some food standing from last evening's meal; this is eaten cold in the forenoon. It is so common that the middle of the forenoon, about 9 a. m., is called the time of (eating) this.

[13] The Santals will always avoid using proper names, using some name denoting relationship or the like instead. Here it is literally "the youngest", viz. son in the family. See the writer's 'Taboo and Customs connected therewith among the Santals', Journal of the Asiatic Society of Bengal, Vol. LXVII, part III. 1898.

[14] See p. 58, note 10.

The young man then said: "Should I tell to get a beating? I should perhaps not have any fear?"

"Well then," she said, "so we have made the matter nice and round."

After this it is difficult to tell what happened to them. They wished always to be together; they were talking something or other, and there they were. The buffaloes were also eating leaves of trees there in the vicinity, and there they stayed. And these two were flirting and dallying the whole time, and he quite forgot to send her home; they stayed in this way until after sunset. Then somehow the boy came to his senses and remembered that it was getting dark. So he said to her: "Hallo, you did not go! With whom will you now be able to go? Come let us go together, then we shall drive these along also. They are surely looking for you to-day at home; my brother will thrash us both to death."

But she replied: "He will not beat us at all. I shall put him off in a moment."

After this talk they drove the buffaloes along. When they reached the end of the village street, she said to him: "I say, small one, now you drive them along, I am going on in advance. I shall like to hear them, what they are angry for. We shall not come there together."

"Get along then," he said to her, and with this he sent her in advance. So from there she took herself off, and then who knows what became of her. But the young man did not know that she was a bonga girl.

This girl now became quite familiar with him. They constantly met, she always in the likeness of his sister-in-law. Sometimes she even awakened him and took him away from home. Still he was not able to make her out. They remained like this for about a whole year.

Then it once happened that she awakened him and took him away from home at midnight. The young man seemed to remember that he went out by the opening leading out to the field in which the house was standing; but then somehow she made him lose sight of realities. Somehow or other she took him away to the rock just above the mango spring, and they were sitting there.

Then after some time the young man came to his senses, he looked and saw the mango trees, the spring and ravines and the rocks and said: "Hallo, where has she taken me to now in the middle of the night? This *hili* of mine is not a good woman." The young man was thinking so with himself.

Then a short while afterwards, they tell, they somehow all at once reached home again, and only after he had slept and awoke again the cock crowed, and then she had disappeared. This matter remained in the young man's mind, and at the time of eating the remainders from last evening's meal[12] he asked his sister-in-law: "Look here, *hili*, where did you take me to last night?"

Adọ uni hilit erae mẹnkeṭa, Okor họ, iń dọ tinreń idileṭmea? Iń dọ okate hõ bạń riạu idi akaṭmea. Ạuṛiakte iń dọ alom dọseńa.

Adọ unreye mẹnkeṭa, Ọkọe cọń, hili, teheń ńindại bereṭ idilidińa hana ul jharna cetan cạṭạnite. Sinạm am lekageye ńẹlokạ, ar rọṛ hõ am lekage, landa hõ am lekage. Onate am dọń kulikam kana, okatem idilidińa mẹnte.

Adọ tiriṭ leka uni dọe mẹnkeṭa, Jọnọmre hõ, huḍińić, iń dọ bạń idi akaṭmea ar bereṭ hõ bạń bereṭ akaṭmea. Ma hoṇẹć sunum sakam ńẹl ocoeme.

Adọe mẹnkeṭa, Baṅa, hili, sunum sakam dọ ọhọń ńẹl ocolea. Am hõ bam lạieṭ khan, ma bogeyena. Tọbẹ khan ọkọe cọe idilidińa.

Ar hilit era dọ tiriṭ lekae metae kana, Baṅa, bạbu, iń dọ baṅgeń idi akaṭmea. Dhorae boṅga kange cọń ceṭ cọń. Unige pasẹn iń chinteye idileṭme.

Adọ uni koṛae mẹnkeṭa, Acha nãhãḱ iń bidạuea. Judi teheń ńindại beredíń khan dọ, bạń calakạ; ar ạḍiye jid khan dọ, ape nãhãḱ iń họhọapea.

Adọe metadea, Ma nãhãḱ họhọeme, dadam iń lạiaea, adọ cirgạlgeliń tahẹna. Adọ inạḱ galmaraokategekin thirena.

Adọ ona katha hilit era dọe lạikeṭa. Metae kanae, Teheń ma bhala huḍińić dọ iń chinte ọkọe cọko bereṭ idiledete hana ul jharna cạṭạnite, kathaeye idiledea. Adọ teheń setaḱ jọkhẹn bogeteye dhora marayedíń kana, amgem idilidińa mẹnte. Adọń metae kana, Henda họ, iń dọ tinreń idileṭmea? Iń thọ bạń disạyeṭa. Ar ceṭ lagaṭ bạń idime? Bam pạṭiạuḱ kan khan, ma ẹnte sunumko boṅga baṛa ocoeme. Adọe mẹnkeṭa, Hẽ, sunum sakam dọ ọhọń ńẹl ocolea. Ẹnte rọṛ hõ landa hõ sinạm am lekage, onate iń dọ amgeń badeṭmea. Adọ arhõe mẹnkeṭa, Acha, tọbẹ khan teheń ńindạ nãhãḱe bẹrẹdíń khan dọń họhọea, adọ gọńeńpe. Adọ unre iń hõń metae kana, Acha besge, họhọeme. Noa katha dọ dadam hõń lạiaea. Adọ bana họṛ jẹmọn cirgạlliń tahẹn. Onate am hõ noa katha dọń lạiam kana, jẹmọnlaṅ disạye.

Adọ uniye lạiade khan, uni dọ sanam họṛ ṭhene sọdọr gọṭkaṭa. Khange ẹn hiloḱ khon sanam họṛ sọntọrko tahẽyena. Arko mẹnkeṭa, Hapẹ bon thir hataṛokạ ar sọntọrbon tahẹna, sạri sẹ naseko bereṭede kana. Ńẹlkoabon sẹbon ańjọmkoa. Adọ inạḱkatege ẹn hiloḱ dọko thir baṛayena. Adọ ạyuṗ ńindạ khange unkinaḱ tak ńẹla mẹnte sanam họṛ cirgạlge menaḱkoa.

Adọ sạri tala ńindạ khange uni boṅga kuṛi dọe hẹć gọṭena. Adọ tinre cọń uni koṛa ṭhene bọlọ gọṭen. Bọloḱ jọkhẹn dọ ọkọe hõ bako disạ bọlọledea. Adọ uni koṛa ṭhene sẹnenteye bereṭede kana, are metae kana, Delaṅ hantẹ bahre sẹnlaṅ oḍokokạ. Adọ bereṭente uni koṛa dọe duṛuṗena, ar rọṛ dọ ceṭ hõ bae rọṛ sạḍeyeṭa. Adọ ọntẹye riạuede kan khan, uni koṛa dọ hilittẹṭe họhọadea. Adọ sạri unkin hõ cirgạlkin tahẽkante, jẹmone họhọleṭa, tẹmọngekin gọń gọṭkedete bereṭ tora divheko jẹrẹṭ marsal gọṭkeṭa. Adọko arsal baṛayede kan dọe ać eskarge. Adọko kulikedea, Henda ya, ceṭ lagaṭem họhọleṭa?

13-14 See p. 88.

15 See p. 92.

"Why," she replied, "when did I take you anywhere? I have not asked you to come anywhere with me. You are putting blame on me without any cause."

"Somebody, *hili*," he then said, "who can know who it was, awakened me to-night and took me to the rock just above that mango spring. Precisely like you she looks; her voice is also like yours; she laughs also like you. Therefore I am asking you where you took me to."

But she persisted in saying: "Not at all, small one[13], I have not taken you anywhere, nor have I awakened you. You should consult the oil-oracle."[14]

"No, *hili*," he replied, "I shall certainly not consult the oil-oracle. As you do not tell either, it is all right. Then somebody else, whoever it was, took me away."

His sister-in-law persisted in saying: "No, my lad, I have not taken you anywhere. It is surely a bonga, or somebody of that kind. Perhaps she took you away in my likeness."

"Well then," the young man replied, "I shall put her to the test presently. If she awakens me to-night, I shall not go, and if she persists, I shall call out to you."

"Do call out," she said, "I shall tell your elder brother, and we two shall be on the watch." Having talked thus much together they stopped.

His sister-in-law told it to her husband and said: "Last night somebody, whoever it was, in my likeness, it seems, awakened the small one and took him, he says, to the rock at the mango spring. This morning he gave me an all-round talking-to and insisted that I had taken him away. I said to him: "Look here, at what time of the night did I take you away? I do not remember it. And why should I take you away? If you don't believe me, please let them consult the oil-oracle." Then he said: "Quite so; I shall certainly not let them consult the oil-oracle. You see, both voice and laugh were exactly like yours; therefore I conclude it is you". Then he again said: "Well then, if she awakens me to-night, I shall call out; then answer me!" So I also said to him: "All right, call out. I shall also let your brother know of this matter." So let us both be on the alert. Therefore I have told you also of this matter, in order that we may keep him in mind."

When she had told him, he at once disclosed it to everybody, and from that time all of them were alert and said: "Wait, we shall keep quiet in the meantime and be on the look-out, whether it is true or not that she awakens him. We shall see them, or hear them." Having said so much they did nothing more that day; but when night fell all of them were on the alert to see what would happen to these two.

At midnight that bonga girl really came and, goodness knows when, went in to the young man; no one was aware of her, when she entered. She went up to the young man, awakened him and said to him: "Come, let us go outside." The young man then got up and sat down; but he did not say a word. But as she proposed to him to go out, the young man called out to his sister-in-law. And as she and her husband were on the alert, as soon as he called out, they answered at once, got up and lighted a lamp[15]. But as they let the light fall on him, it was he alone they saw. Then they asked him: "Look here, lad, what did you call out for?"

Adoe menketa, Okoe coe dhaka beretkidiña, onaten hohoketa.

Adoko metadea, Ukuriće okayena?

Adoe metatkoa, Noa divhepe jered jokhengeye oka seć goten con.

Ado bako ñamlede khan, divhe doko iríćkatteko gitić barayena. Khange arhõ uni doe hećenteye beretkedea. Adoe metae kana, Teheń dom laikidiña.

Ado uniye menketa, Hẽ, ente am dom okoe kan coń. Hilin iń kulikedea, ado okore godaolena? Uni khan huteć, bae angockea? Ado okore angocleta? Onaten botorenten lai akatgea. Ar ente am hõ nun din andhategem idiyedin kana. Okoe kan com? Cedak ente bam sodorok kana?

Ar uni kora do sanam hore beret ocokoa mente onekin galmarao jokhen do ăt ńoktegeye roret kana. Ado ona ror añjomte apat haram do adi garteye ror sade gotketa. Are ror gotketa, Henda ya, okoe tuluć noa ñinda dom galmarao kana?

Khange ado bana hor cal culkin thir bara gotena. Arhõ divhe jeretkateko ñel barakede doe kora eskarge. Adoe kulikedea, Henda ya, okoe tulućem galmarao kan tahẽkana?

Ado uniye menketa, Mit hor okoe coe hećlena. Ado noa divheyem jered jokhengeye oka seć goten con.

Ado onka bar dhaoteko arsalkedere hõ bako ñam dareadete divhe do mit jeretgeko dohoketa, ado ghuriạ en hilok do bae hećlena. Khange uni bonga kuri doe usat calaoena, ado bae hec ruarlena.

Ado dosar hilok gupi then dosra kuri chinteye sodorena. Ado uni kora bulau aguye lagat adi bariće serenet kana. Ado ona seren añjomte uni kora do uni kuri thene sen sorena.

Ado un jokhen ona ñinda reak katha uni kuri doe sodorketa. Adoe metae kana, Henda pera, ñel thiken kanam?

Adoe menketa, Bań.

Arhõe menketa, Inge con hola ñinda do am then iń senlen. Ado tinre com lai hatar akatte hohoket torage jham jhum joto horko ñir beret goten.

Ado uni korae menketa, Am hõ ente jaogem andha idiń kan do. Mon menaktam khan, bam sodoroka? Cedak hilin bheskate dom calak kana? Ado one ñindage dhiri catanitelan senlen, ona kathage uni do bań kulikedea? Ado bangeye godaok kan. Khange thoń dhakwata ar iń monreń menketa, Durre! okoe endekhane idilidiña? Unre noa katha do sodorena. Ar am hõ ente, un din khon menaklaña, enre hõ noa katha do bam bhedadiña. Ado andha hor cekaten badaea? Ado oneko arsal barame utarle badaeketa, nui doe nonkan hor kana mente do.

---

[15] The lamp is a very primitive affair, an oil-container, formerly generally of earthenware, with a thick thread as a wick. All kinds of vegetable oils were used. Petroleum lamps are a later introduction.

[16] All places here referred to are in the northern part of the Santal Parganas district, where there is an English mission.

[17] The bonga girl uses the name, which is against all custom with a woman and here is meant to show how angry she is.

"Somebody," he replied, "whoever it was, pushed me and got me up; therefore I called out."

"We don't see anybody," they said, "what became of her?"

"When you lighted the lamp," he replied, "she suddenly disappeared somewhere."

As they did not find her, they put out the light and went to bed. Then that bonga girl came again and got him up and said to him: "To-day you have told them about me."

"Yes," he answered, "because you are who knows who. I questioned my *hili*; but would she admit it? If it was she, would not she confess it to me? But did she? Not at all. Then I became afraid and told them. You see, you have also now so long a time been taking me away without my understanding what it is. Who are you? Why don't you show yourself?"

In order to make everybody in the house get up the young man was talking rather loudly, when they were speaking together. When his old father heard them talking, he at once called out in a very loud voice, and said: "Look here, my lad, with whom are you talking now in the night?"

Then both of them stopped talking and were silent. Again they lighted a lamp and let the light fall on the young man, and they saw it was he alone. Then the old man asked him: "Look here, my lad, who is it with whom you were talking?"

"Somebody," he replied, "came, I don't know who. When you lighted this lamp, she disappeared somewhere."

As they had searched for her with lighted lamp twice without being able to find her, they let the lamp stand there burning, and she did not come any more that night. The bonga girl went away sulking and did not return.

The next day she showed herself in the likeness of another girl, where they were herding cattle. In order to entice the young man away, the bonga girl was singing all she could, and as the young man heard that singing, he went near to the girl, and they started talking and flirting. Now the girl disclosed what had happened in the night, and said to the boy: "Look here, my friend, do you recognize me?"

"No," he replied.

"Why," she said, "it was I who went to you yesterday night. But as you some time before had told them, all of them got up with a rush, as soon as they were called out."

"Well," the boy replied, "you have all along been deceiving me. If you are so minded, will you not disclose yourself? Why do you go about in the form of my sister-in-law? You remember, when we two at night went to that rock, — did not I ask her about that? But she would not in any way acknowledge it. Then I got nettled at this and said to myself: "O dear, who then did take me away?" Then this matter was brought to light. You see, we two have been together for so long a time; still you have never let me know. And I am ignorant of the truth; how should I know? When they were seeking for you with a lighted lamp, then only we understood that you were something like this."

Adǫ kathae, ẹn hiloḱ dǫ menaḱkinge; ńindạyenre hõ ǫṇḍege menaḱkin. Ar kaḍa bitkil dǫ akotege oṛaḱteko calaoena. Ar nui koṛa dǫ uni kuṛige ako oṛaḱteye idikedea. Adǫ mit́ ńindạ ǫṇḍẹge dǫhǫ aṅgakate dosar hiloḱ dǫe kol gǫt́kadea. Khange uni koṛa dǫ bhạgte oṛaḱe hẹćlena. Adǫ hẹć torako kuli baṛakedea, okarem tahẽkana mẹnte. Adǫe lạikeṭa, baṅma, Uni ńindại hẹćlen kuṛigeye ńamkidińte ać ṭhene dǫhǫ aṅgakidińa. Nẽkẽ ẹṇḍẹ khon nitgeń hijuḱ kana.

Ar uni koṛa mǫnre dǫe dhik caba akana, mẹnkhan noa katha dǫ ǫkǫe hõ bae lạiako kana. Adǫ dakakoe jǫm baṛaketa, adǫ kaḍa ṭhen calaḱ lekageye sapṛao oḍok gǫt́ena. Adǫ kaḍa ṭhen hõ bae sẹnlena; ẹkkalte Taljhạri Misonte ǫloḱ ced lagat́e calaoena. Are mẹnketa, Nun sạṅgiń dǫ jạnić ǫhǫe hijuḱa. Adǫ thoṛa thuṛi ǫloḱ iń cetle khan dǫń um dapoṛoḱa.

Ar uni koṛa ma ǫntẹye calaoen, ar ǫkǫe hõ bae lại oṭoat́koa, iń dǫ nǫtẹ sẹ ǫntẹń calaḱ kana mẹnte. Adǫ bae lạilet́ karǫnte oṛaḱren dǫko ãonda ạundi baṛae kana. Adǫko mẹnketa, Ǫhǫbo ńamlea; dhora uni boṅga kuṛigeye aṅgẹnkedetabona. Adǫ onkako hudisket́te sunum sakam bogeteko ńẹl baṛa ocoyeta. Adǫ okare hõ bako khǫṛǫ daṛeae kana.

Adǫ khange uni boṅga kuṛi dǫ cekate cǫe baḍaeket́, baṅma, haṇḍegeye sẹnakana mẹnte. Ar sẹ uni koṛa dǫ ǫṇḍẹ sẹnkate mǫṭhẹ pẹ candogeye hoe akan tahẽkana. Khange uni boṅga kuṛi dǫe pańja gǫt́kedea. Adǫe metae kana, Am dǫ iń bǫtǫrtege nǫṇḍẹ dǫm hẹć akana. Adǫ am paḱńjage iń dǫń hẹć akana. Adǫ celem calaḱa sẹ baṅ? Ma, cet́em mẹneta? Rǫṛme.

Adǫ uni koṛa dǫ ạurigeye ạṇḍuń baṛayeta. Mẹnet́ae, Calao mań calaokoḱge. Sahebge thǫ ǫhǫe chuṭilińa.

Adǫ uniye mẹnketa, Ma ẹnte metaeme. Chuṭi baṅkhane cekamea? Do nãhãḱ calaḱte metaeme.

Adǫ koṛae mẹnketa, Durrẹ! lajao paṛa. Nẹtargeń bhorti akana, arhõ chuṭiń kǫeye khan, bae edreańa? Baṅa, nịạ dhao dǫ sẹn ruạroḱme, baṅ calaḱ kana. Arhõ pẹ cando gan iń paṛhaolẹnge, adǫń calao utạroḱa, adǫ am ṭhengeń tahẹna.

Adǫ kuṛiye mẹnketa, Tǫbẹ khan ǫhǫm sẹnlena?

Adǫe mẹnketa, Hẽ, nịạ dhao dǫ baṅ calaḱ kana.

Adǫ kuṛiye mẹn oṭokata, Cet́, phalna, calaḱ bam rẹbẹn kana? Ńẹlam nãhãḱ, am dǫ ińaḱ katha bam dǫhǫyeta, ona reaḱ dǫm aṭkara nãhãḱ.

Adǫ enka mẹnkategẹ uni kuṛi dǫe hẹćena. Adǫ uni hẹćate mit́ candoge hoelena, khange uni koṛae koṅkayena. Cet́ko cǫń ạl mạl rǫṛe ẹhǫṕketa. Paṛhao hõ besgeye ẹhǫba, tayǫmte khan cet́ko cǫń bhacka bhạcki ạurigeye paṛhaoa. Adǫko ruhedere hõ bae bataoa. Arhõ oka dǫ onkogeye besaokoa.

---

[16] [17] See p. 92.

[18] Such madness as here described is generally thought to be due to the influence of evil spirits. The Santali word here translated "nonsensical" is often used about gibberish, inane and obscene talk, considered insane.

[19] See p. 58, note 10.

That day they remained there; when night came, they still stayed on. The buffaloes went home of their own accord, and the girl took this young man with her to their house, kept him there for the whole night and then sent him away. The young man fortunately found his way home. As soon as he arrived, they questioned him where he had been. He then told them: "The girl that came at night met with me and kept me with her until dawn. Just now at this moment I am coming from there."

The young man was feeling disgusted; but he did not tell anybody of this. They took their meal, whereupon he made himself ready and went out, as if he were going to the buffaloes. He did not, however, do that; he went straight to the Taljhari Mission[16] to learn to write, thinking: "The girl will not be likely to come so far, and when I have learnt to write a little, I shall be baptized."

The young man went there, and he did not, before leaving, tell anybody that he was going to this or that place. As he did not tell, his relatives were searching everywhere for him. At last they said: "We shall never find him; surely, that bonga girl has spirited our boy away." Thinking this they consulted the oil-oracle over and over again; but they were not able to find any trace of him anywhere.

The bonga girl, however, somehow or other got to know, that he had gone to that place. At the time only three months had passed since he went there. The bonga girl thereupon followed after him, found him and said to him: "It is because you are afraid of me that you have come here. So I have come to trace you. Now, what will you do, will you come along or not? What will you do? Speak."

The young man came with some trivial excuses and said: "I might be willing to go; but the Saheb will certainly not give me leave."

"Well," she replied, "tell him you will leave. What else should he do than give you free? Do go at once and speak to him."

"O dear me," the boy said, "it is a shame. It is only a short time since I have been taken on; if I now ask him for leave, will he not be angry with me? No, go back again this time; I am not going with you. Let me read three months more; then I shall go away for good and remain with you."

"You are then quite unwilling to go?" the girl asked him.

"Yes," he replied, "this time I am not going."

The girl then said, as she left: "What, you so and so[17]! you refuse to come? You will see presently; you will not do as I say; you will feel the result presently."

Having said this the girl came away. About a month later the boy became mad[18]. He commenced to talk all kinds of nonsense. He would start reading all right; then he would read on some gibberish, and when they scolded him, he would not heed. Now and then he also mimicked the teachers.

---

[20] See p. 50, note 9. After having been properly driven away she is supposed not to be able to come back

Khange Sahebe mẹnkeťa, Ma tọlepe, ranbo emaea. Khange tọlkedete ranko emadea. Adọ inạkate khange uni kọṛa dọe ńir baṛae kana. Adọ onka ńir ńirte ako oṛaḱteye ńir hẹćena. Ẹkkalte ona ul jharnategeye ńir calaḱa. Adọ ọṇḍeye sẹnlen khane besenge, ar oṛaḱre khan, ceťko cọń ạḍiye harmadkoa. Ar jọm hõ bae jọma, osoḱ rọhọrenae.

Khange eńgat apat dọ ojhakin saṕkeťkoteko husiťkedea. Uni bọńga kuṛiko lagakedea sẹko bidạwadea. Khange uni koṛae besena, adọ ghuriạ̃ uni kuṛi dọ koṛa ṭhen bae hẹć daṛeaťa.

Adọ ẹnẹye bes utạrente arhõ ọloḱgeye calaoente ọṇḍegeye tahẽyenteye umena, ar ọṇḍegeye baplayenteye oḍokena. Kạmiko emadete nit hạbić Purọḍhạmni bańglare kạmi kan menaegea. Ar nitkate dọ jọtọ garọsṭi sudhạko um cabayena.

Noa dọ ńẹlaḱ katha kana, kạhni eman dọ bań kana. Ọkọe hoṛ tuluć bọńga kuṛiye tahẽkana, uni hoṛ hõ nit hạbić menaegea, ar nui Jamkandọrren koṛa hõ menaegea. Ọkọe hoṛko gọćena, onkanaḱ dọ kạhniko metaḱ kana. Ar onkan kạhni lekan katha dọ pẹə ponea gan menaḱa. Adọ mẹnkhan onkanaḱ dọ bań ọlleťa. Ar adọm katha dọ okako ṭhen dọ noakin tuluć midoḱgea ar miť bar ṭhen dọ begaroḱgea.

Ar noko kuṛi họpọn jạt dọ cekate cọń algategeko bulạu gọdoḱgea, hoṛ kuṛi sẹ bọńga kuṛi. Ńẹlme, nui dọ tirio ọrọńteye lọbena. Hoṛ kuṛi hõko lọboḱ kangea. Ar banamte ar sereńte, ḍọm ẹnẹćte, nonka bin ạksulaḱ jinisteko bulạuḱ kana. Adọ ma sẹ bujme ẹnte, tirio ọrọń ar banam sereńte dọ bań ạksula. Miťṭań ona dọ jut ańjọmoḱ kana, inạge; ar bańkhan onate jähān lab bạnuḱan. Adọ ọkọe bako buj ṭhikeť kuṛiko bulạuḱ kana. Metaḱme onako orad dọ bạnuḱtakoa onkan hoṛ. Adọ ẹnẹ nią katha dọ cabayena.

Adọ koṛa bọńga reaḱ katha. Miťṭań kamar ạimại din hiloḱ ạḍiye rọť nạkijoḱ are misiḱ kan tahẽkana, ar bojawaḱ mithi sunume ọjọkeť tahẽkana. Khange bọńga koṛa dọe bulạu gọṭena.

Miť dinoḱ uni kamar hẹrẹl dọ peṛa họroḱe calaoena, adọ ruạṛageye mẹnleťa. Adọ ceť bẹoṛa· iạte cọń bae ruạṛlena. Ar gidrạtakin dọko pẹaḱgea. Adọ ạyuṕ ńindạyen hõ bae ruạṛlena, ar nuiye hijuḱa mẹnte gitić gọrọ hoṛ bako ạguleťkoa.

Adọ tala ńindạ khange uni bọńga hẹrẹl dọ kamar hẹrẹl chinteye hẹć gọṭenteye họhọ sạḍeketa. Adọko jhićadeteye bọlọyena. Dakako ẹm gelawade, bae jọmleťa. Mẹnketae, Bi akangeań. Adọ ẹnẹko jaegayente ạkin dọ haṛam buḍhi reaḱkin kajeťa. Adọ unre thoṛa dọe aṭkar oromledegea, mẹnkhan unre dọ ceť hõ bae rọṛ sạḍeleťa. Ẹnte rọṛ landa aṛańko ma sinạm ać hẹrẹlaḱ lekage, onate bae phuṭleťa. Adọ miť ńindạkin kaj ańgaketa. Adọ setaḱ khangeye okayen cọń. Adọ un utạre dhakwaťa. Mẹnketae, Ọhrẹ! apatteť dọe bań kana. Apate tahẹn khan, nit dọe okaḱa? Bae tahẽkoḱa?

19 20 See p. 94 – 95.

21 It is of seldom occurrence, but the writer has met several persons who have wanted to be baptized, because they have believed that this will save them from the power of the evil spirits. Even heathen may be heard to advise other people to turn Christians in order to be saved from witches or malicious **bońgas**, when they have tried all remedies known to them without effect.

22 See commencement of this section. Here the Santal writer seems to make some reservations, as if he would not personally vouch for all he tells. He has undoubtedly a strong belief in the possibility.

23 25 See pp. 98 99.

Then the Saheb said: "Bind him, we shall give him medicine." So they tied him up and gave him medicine. After this had been done, the young man ran away; and running from place to place he reached his own home. There he would run straight to the mango spring, and when he reached there he was well; but when he was at home, he would do his people all kinds of mischief. He would not eat either and became lean and emaciated.

Thereupon his parents applied to some *ojhas*[19] and exorcized him. They drove the bonga girl away, i. e., they gave her her dismissal[20]. The young man then became well, and the girl could not return any more to the boy.

As he now in this way entirely recovered, he again went to learn to write, and staying there he was ultimately baptized[21], and having married he came out of the school. They gave him work, and he is still working at the Purodhamni bungalow. Now by this time the whole family has been baptized.

This is what has been seen; it is not a story[22]. The man with whom the bonga girl lived, that man is still living. The young man from Jamkandor is also still alive. What is told about dead people, such tales they call folk-tales, and there are some three or four tales of that kind; but such ones I have not written here. Here and there these tales agree with what has been told in these two stories; in a few places they are different.

Now girls[23] somehow or other are so easily led astray, whether they are human girls or bonga girls. Observe, this one was led astray through flute playing. Human girls are also led astray. Through fiddle playing and song, through dancing, through anything which has no value to support people, they are led astray. Understand, flute playing and fiddling and singing does not support us. It is nice to hear, that is all; otherwise there is no profit by such things. And those girls who do not understand it properly, they are led astray. That is to say, such people as have no proper estimation of these matters. So there is an end to this tale.

Then there is something about male bongas. There was a blacksmith[24] woman who was in the habit of daily combing and tying up her hair and blackening her teeth; she also anointed herself with the finest scented oil. Then there was a bonga who became enamoured of her.

One day the blacksmith went on a visit to friends, intending to come back that day; but delayed by something or other he did not return. They had three children. It became evening and night, still he did not return, and as they expected him back again, they did not bring anybody to stay the night with them[25].

At midnight the bonga came in the likeness of the blacksmith and called out. They opened to him and he came in. They put food before him, but he did not eat. "I have had food," he said. Hereupon they went to bed. She felt a little uncertain whether he was her husband, but did not say anything, because his voice and manner was so exactly like that of her husband. As soon as it was morning, he disappeared. Then only she understood. "Oh", she said, "he is not father. If he were he, where should he now go off to? Would he not stay?"

Adọ dosar hilokko ńẹl hor̥kede. Dosar hilok hõ bae hẹćlen. Adọ mitṭań buḍhi hor̥ gitić gor̥oko idikedete bhitri khọn rẹnd bẹndko esẹtena arko hurkạr̥ tirupena.

Adọ kathae, tala ńindą khange arhõe hẹć gọtena are họhọ sạḍe gọtketa. Khange kathae, bọtor̥te jọtọ hor̥ko beretena, divheko jẹrẹtketa, adọ bako jhićae kana. Khange ạdi garteye ruhẹt gọtketa, Ma hare phare jhić họtańpe. Adọ bako jhićet khan dọ, silpińe ḍhaka rạput gọtketteye bọlọ gọtente uni ạimạiye sap gọtkedea, ar mạt mạte tọgọć ḍạtawae kana, ar pọnḍge jolok lekae bẹńgẹtae kana. Khange uni dọe kẹklẹsẹtena ar sanam hor̥geko kẹklẹsẹtenteko haemoekạtena. Adọe kar̥go bindạr̥ gọtkedete khub lekae dalkedea, kathae, hãkar hãkar alańge ọḍokentaea. Ar mọkọń tora pandeye lẹbẹt ọṭokadea.

Khange uni ạimại dọe kub kubu utạrena ar ḍhelak ḍhelak mãyãmgeye ulạyeta, ar ror̥ dọ atentaea. Baskeak ber khange kamar herẹle hẹćena, adọ ini tulućgeye ńẹpellena. Mit dhaoe bẹńgẹt rakapadea, adọ jivi calaoentaea.

Ar uni kamar herẹl dọe kuli bar̥aketko khan, sanam bhẹdko lại̥ade khan dọ kaḍa lekae adrao gọtketa. Adọ ẹnte rakkate hõe cekaea? Gọćen hor̥ dọ okarem ńamea? Adọ ẹnẹko oḍok idikedeteko ḍahọnkedea. Adọ inạkate pẹ pon mãhã khange uni kamar dọ ọnḍẹ khone dạr̥keta.

Ar uni bońga herẹl ma iną pande lẹbẹt ọṭokategẹye calaoen. Adọ ọnẹ onka saj ar cõhõkok khan dọ, bońga herẹl hõko lọbokgea. Nią dọ ańjom katha kana. Ọnẹ adọ bońga ar hor̥ko baplak kan reak sẹko lọtghuṭi akat reak katha. Adọ nịare pẹ hor̥ak kathań lại̥keta sẹń ọlketa. Adọń mucạtketa.

Adọ ẹnẹ cabayena katha dọ.

9. Hor̥ boṅgako tulućko bapla akan reak katha

Hor̥ ar bońga disomre ḍher hor̥ko bapla akańgea, mẹnkhan sọdọr̥ bapla thọ bań kana. Ato hor̥ sẹ disom hor̥ dur̥up tẹńgoak, onage sọdọr̥ sẹ sạbik bapla dọko metak kana, sẹ asọl bapla dọ ona kangea. Ar akote ńapamkateko baplak kan, ona dọ asọl bapla dọ bako metak kana. Adọ arhõ noa bońga ar hor̥ bapla akan reak kathage arhõń lại̥yeta; metakme ona dọ nonka kana.

Hana Silṅgi sẹnak Dọrbar atore bar hor̥ bońga kurikin bạhuan tahẽkana. Mitṭań dọ tirio ạḍiye ọrọńet tahẽkante onateye bulạuledea. Kaḍa gasao jọkhẹn hor̥ kur̥i chinte uni ṭhene sẹnlena. Unrekin ńapamente uni kor̥a tulućе gateyena.

---

23 Santals, like all orientals, have small faith in women, especially in their morality. In spite of this the Santal woman has often a very good position in Santal society, and just as often as not it is the woman who rules the household and often — indirectly — the village.

24 The Santals keep a blacksmith in the village, or two or three villages may keep one together. He makes and repairs all agricultural implements used by them, sharpens axes and so on, being paid a certain amount of paddy for each plough used by the people. The Santals call these blacksmiths *kamar;* they generally speak a low kind of Hindi or Bihari, besides a little Santali. They are generally styled semi-hinduized aboriginals, whatever their origin may be.

Next day they waited for the husband; that day he did not come either. So they brought an old woman to stay during the night with them, shut up the house entirely from inside and put bars to the door.

Then, they tell, at midnight the bonga came again and called out. In fear and trembling all of them got up and lighted a lamp; but they did not open to him. Then he started scolding in a loud voice: "Be quick, open to me at once!" As they did not open, he pushed the door and broke it, came in and at once took hold of the woman and gnashed his teeth at her; he was looking at her, his eyes white and like blazing. She was frightened out of her wits, so they were all of them, and became stiff like logs from fear. Thereupon he threw her down on the floor and beat her, while he was wheezing and his tongue was hanging out of his mouth[26]. Then he kicked her in her stomach and left.

Thereupon the woman was utterly bent up and was vomiting clots of blood, and lost her speech. In the middle of the forenoon her husband came, so she met with him. She looked up at him once; then her soul left her[27].

When the blacksmith questioned them, and they had told him what it all meant, he bellowed like a buffalo. But what could he do crying? Where can you find a dead person? They took her body out and burnt it. Some three or four days afterwards the blacksmith went away from there for good.

The bonga went away after having kicked her. In this way, when women put on ornaments and make themselves beautiful, male bongas also are allured. This is a story I have heard. This was about bongas and human beings having married or been living together. Here I have written about three such cases. There it is ended.

There now, that is the end of the tale.

9. MORE TALES ABOUT SANTALS MARRIED WITH BONGAS

Many Santals[1] and *bongas* have married in this country; but, of course, it has not been public marriages. When the village people[2] or the country people attend the ceremonies, then it is called a public or real marriage; that is the genuine marriage. When people meet and marry by themselves, people do not call this a real marriage. Here I shall again tell some stories about Santals and bongas having married.

In the village of Dorbar near Silingi[3] two men had taken bonga girls for their wives. One of them was in the constant habit of playing the flute, and thereby he led the bonga girl astray. While he was one day washing the buffaloes, she went up to him in the likeness of a Santal girl. After they had met that time, she became intimate with the young man.

---

[25] It is customary with Santals and others, when the males of a house leave for a short absence, to call in somebody to stay for the night, both as a kind of protection and out of consideration for the Santal Mrs. Grundy.

[26] What is described here, seems to point to a suspicion that the *bonga* is a kind of wild animal.

[27] A common Santali expression. The soul is thought at death to leave its hut, as the body is often called.

[1–3] See p. 100.

Adọ mõṛẽ turui māhā gatekate mit́ din dọ uni kuṛiye mẹnketa, Dela teheń dọ ale oṛak̃teń idimea. Inạ dọ ale oṛak̃em ńẹl ạguitalea.

Adọ uni koṛae mẹnketa, Kạḍa nāhāk̃ko adok̃tiṅa.

Adọe mẹnketa, Baṅa, nāhāk̃ mit́ ghạṛitem hẹć gọdok̃a. Kạḍa dọ nẹṇḍẹge tahẽ ocoako; ọhọko okatek̃tama.

Adọ arhõe metadea, Sẹn mań sẹnkok̃ge; pasẹ ape oṛak̃ren cet́ko metań. Onage thọ lajaogeń metak̃ kana.

Adọ uniye mẹnketa, Ọhọko metama. Do nāhāk̃ jāhānak̃ko metam khan, ińiń dok̃mea. Khange adọ ẹnẹkin calaoena. Khange uni kuṛiren apat eṅgat dọ kuṛiko kulikedea, Henda mạị, nui dọ ọkọeyem ạyur ạgukedea?

Adọe metat́koa, Jāwāe kanae.

Khange adọ duṛup̃ lạgit́ hapṛak̃ hapṛak̃ biṅko piti akana; ona dọ, kathae, gaṇḍo kantakoa. Adọ onko biṅge mitṭaṅko sọhọr gọtkadea arko metadea, Ma jāwāe, ona gaṇḍore duṛup̃ben.

Adọ kathae, nui koṛa dọ bọtọrte uni biń gaṇḍore dọ bae duṛup̃lena, ọtregeye duṛup̃ena. Adọ duṛup̃kate ọntẹ nọtẹ beṛhaeteye bẹṅgẹt́ baṛayet́ khan dọe ńẹlet́ko dọ, aema utạr biṅko dọhọ akat́ko arko piṭi baṛa akan. Arhõ mit́ sẹnre dọ kul tạrup̃ aema utạrko burum baṛa akan sẹko ọbọr baṛa akane ńẹlket́koa. Khange thọ bẹbạṛiće bọtọrok̃ kana are mẹneta, Durrẹ! cet́ gara eṅgateń hẹćena? Adọ onka bogeteye bọtọrok̃ kana. Khange dạṛe mẹnjoń kanre ma họr bae disạyet́ kan, oka sẹnteye dạṛa. Are mẹneta, Dhorage noko kul tạrup̃ ṭhen dọko jọm ocoṅgea nāhāk̃. Ar nui tuluć dọ cet́ hõ bako rọṛ baṛayeta; nui dọ ać eskar pharakreye duṛup̃ akana. Adọ māyāk̃ mõyõk̃geye ạikạueta. Ar uni kuṛi hõ oṛak̃ bhitri sẹnrege cet́ko cọe ceka baṛayet́ kante nui ṭhen dọ bae sorok̃ kana. Koṛa dọ mọnẹ mọnẹteye mẹnjoń kana, Cekate bań bae hijuk̃ kan? Hẹćlen khan iń mẹnkea, Delań, idi ọṭokaṅme mẹnte. Adọ bae sorok̃ kante nui dọ kirdhume duṛup̃ thir akangea.

Adọ sạri inạ mit́ ghạṛi khangeye oḍok gọtena. Khange adọe gạvić gọtadea. Adọ uni kuṛiye hẹć sorena. Adọe metae kana, Cele cet́ lagat́em họhọań kana?

Adọe metadea, Cet́ hõ bań; oṛak̃ ńẹlem ạgulidiṅa, adọń ńẹl baṛaket́tapea. Adọ delań, họr uduk̃ gọtaṅme, calak̃ań. Kạḍa nāhāk̃ko okatek̃ kan cọń.

Adọe metadea, Hapẹ, mit́ ghạṛi thir hataṛok̃me; am lagat́geń pikṭhạ kana. Inań isinle khange nāhāk̃ jọm baṛakatelań calak̃a.

Adọe metadea, Ma ẹnḍẹkhan hako pako usạra gọdme.

Adọ sạri hare phare ini mọtọ lạgit́ko isin laha gọtket́a. Adọ jọm lạgit́ dak̃e taṅadea are metadea, Ma ạbukok̃me; jọm baṛakatelań calak̃a.

---

[1] It might be noted that the Santal name for a human being and for a Santal is the same.

[2] While the binding part of the marriage ceremony is the act of the man, i. e. the bridegroom, putting *sindur* on the forehead of the girl, no marriage is considered a real one without the public having been present. The village headman as a representative of society must be there. See p. 59, note 2, p. 67, note 7.

[3] Silingi is a place in the so-called Dumka Damin, to the north east of Dumka, the headquarters of the Santal Parganas district.

[4–5] See p. 102.

After they had been intimate for five or six days, the girl one day said: "Come along, to-day I shall take you to our home, so you can see where we live."

"My buffaloes will be lost," the young man replied.

"Oh no," she said, "in a moment you will be back here. Let the buffaloes stay here; they will certainly not go anywhere away from you."

"Well," the young man said, "I should like to go; but perhaps your people might say something to me. That I feel ashamed of."

"They will surely not say anything to you," she replied. "Do come; if they should say anything to you, I shall stand up for you."

Thereupon they went[4]. When they had arrived, the girl's parents asked her: "Look here, our girl, who is this whom you have brought along."

"He is my husband," she answered them.

Now, to sit on they had big, big snakes coiled up[5]. These, people tell, are their stools. They pushed one of these snakes towards him, saying: "Please, son-in-law, sit down on this stool."

But the young man was afraid and did not sit down on the snake-stool; he sat down on the ground. Sitting down there he looked round in all directions and saw, look and behold, they were keeping an immense number of snakes which were coiled up. In one direction he further saw a large number of tigers and leopards lying or squatting about. At this he became very much frightened and said to himself: "Dear me, dash it, what sort of evil have I fallen into?" In this way, he was very much afraid; but when he thought of running away, he could not remember the way, so in which direction should he run? He was thinking: "Surely, they will let these tigers and leopards eat me presently." No one spoke to him a single word. He was sitting alone by himself some distance off, staring about and feeling at his wit's end. The girl was also occupied with something or other inside the house and did not come near to him. The young man was saying to himself: "How can it be that she does not come? If she would only come, I should say to her: Come, take me back again." But as she did not come near to him, he was sitting there quietly, hanging his head.

Then, after a while, the girl really came out, and he beckoned to her. She came up to him and asked him: "Well, what is it? What are you calling me for?"

"Oh, it's nothing," he replied, "you brought me here to see your home; now I have seen how you are living. Please come along, show me the way, I must go. The buffaloes will by this time be going astray."

"Wait," she said, "just be quiet a moment. I am making some cakes for you. When I get those ready and you have eaten, you and I shall go at once."

"Well then," he replied, "hurry up and be quick."

Thereupon they quickly prepared some food for him alone. The girl brought him water, saying: "Please, wash your hands; when you have had food, you and I shall go."

Adoe menketa, Bań jometa. Den nondege aguime; idi toraeań; hanteregeń joma.

Khange kuri do boloyente eṅgatteṭ noa kathae laiadea, baṅma, Nonde jom do bae reben kana; idi toraye meneta.

Ado eṅgattete menketa, Baṅa, idi lagaṭ do judategebo emaea. Mae abuk hijuk ma. Ina do orak hõe ńelkatabona.

Khange kuri do arhõ heckateye metae kana, Ma abukokme; jomlem. Idi lagaṭ do judagele emama. Orak ńela menteń aguketmea, ado tobe okor cet lekam ńelkettalea? Ayoe meneta, Mae hijuk ma bare.

Ado onka adiye jidkede khan do, sariye abukenteye ayur aderkedea. Ado ona biń gandogeko beladea. Ado onare do botorte bae duruplena, otregeye durupena. Ado dahe taben gurko emadea, ado lohotkateye sipi jomketa.

Ado onae jojom jokhenge kuriren eṅgatteṭ doe galmaraoae kana. Metae kanae, Nõkõe, jäwäe, orak duar ńel hoponerań doe ayur agu akatbena. Ado ma ńeltaleben. Onate orakte dole hohoaben kana, baṅkhanben menkea, Bhitri sen do cet lekan coṅ, eken bahre khonge sarimtetkogeń ńelkettapea. Ado ma nõkõe ńeltaleben.

Ado sari orakkoe benget barawak kan do, bogete asec tasec cij menaktako, ar Sahebak leka se raj rapajko leka asbab menaktako. Ado jom barakateye odokena. Apat haram do hukai conda aguketa, ado bana horkin ńũ baraketa.

Ado kuriye menketa, Cele, ado delań iń idi otokama. Ado tala hatak gan taben ar pe ganda pithai aguketteye metadea, Ne, ma ghetme, ar delań iń idi otokama.

Ado sari kicricre inakoe ghetketa. Ado eneye agu otokadea; ar uni kuri doe ruarena.

Ado mittań gate kora ona pitha taben do emaea mente uni thene idiketa. Adoe metae kana, Ne ya, pitha tabenem jom khan doń agu akata.

Ado onkae menket khan, uni doe menketa, Den yań joma. Ado rarakatekin ńelet kan do bań kan; taben do meral sakamena, ar pitha do gõethayena. Khan endegekin chitiau gidikata; jom hõ bakin jomleta.

Ado unre uni gatet korae menketa, Am do ya, bejäe phasiara hor kanam. Meral sakam ar gõetham jom ocoń kan do. Noa lagatem hohoań kana?

Ado uniye menketa, Baṅa ya, pitha taben menteged ghet aguleta, ar adom do ondegeń jomketa. Ado cekate coṅ nonkayen, ona do ohoń menlea.

---

[4] It is notable that this story has no mention of the parties passing through water to reach the other side.

[5] See p. 54, note 3.

[6] See p. 54, note 4, p. 55, note 5, p. 81, note 6. Molasses, in Santali called g u r, is the produce of the first inspissation of the juice of the sugar cane, now generally bought in the shops, but also sometimes prepared by the Santals themselves. It is used together with t a h e n and k h a j a r i (see below), and also otherwise, and is the common form of sugar used.

[7] H u k a is the hubble-bubble, a water-bowl — commonly made of the shell of the cocoa-nut, furnished with a stem, on the top of which is an earthenware c i l i m, the head of the pipe. Here the tobacco is put and on top of this a live coal. The smoke is "sucked" out through a hole in the cocoanut. There is, of course, a large number of varieties and elaborately constructed hubble-bubbles, e. g., with long pipes instead of the single hole for

"I shall not eat," he replied: "do bring it here; I shall take it away with me and eat it over there."

The girl went in and told her mother this, saying: "He does not wish to eat here; he wants to take it away with him."

"No," her mother replied, "that will not do; we shall give him separately to take away with him. Let him wash his hands and come. Then he can see our house at the same time."

The girl came back to him again and said to him: "Do wash your hands and take food. We shall give you something else to take away with you. I brought you here, that you might see our house. But in which way have you seen how we live? Why, you have not. Mother says: Let him come."

When she persisted in this way, he finally washed his hands, and the girl took him into the house. They put that snake stool before him; but he was afraid of sitting on it, so he sat down on the ground. Thereupon they brought him curds and taben and molasses[6], and he mixed and ate.

While he was eating, the girl's mother was talking to him. "You see, son-in-law," she said, "my daughter has brought you here to see our house and circumstances. Now please look, how we are living. That is why we have called you into the house. Otherwise you might say: "Who knows how it is inside? It is only the roof I have seen from outside." So now look how it is with us."

He then looked at the house and everything there, it was exuberantly full of things, and they had furniture like that of a saheb or like princes. Having finished eating he came out, and the old father lighted a *huka*[7] and brought it, whereupon they both had a smoke.

Then the girl said: "How is it? Come now and I shall take you back." She brought a winnowing fan[8] half full of *taben* and a dozen cakes, saying: "Please, tie this up; come now, and I shall see you back."

He did so and tied it up in his clothes, whereupon the girl brought him back, while she herself returned.

The young man now took the taben and the cakes to a friend of his to give it to him, saying to him: "Here you, if you like to eat taben and cakes, I have brought some." As he said this, the other replied: "Give it then, I will eat." When they had opened the bundle, they saw it was nothing of the kind: the taben had become *meral*[9] leaves, and the cakes dried cow-dung. So then and there they threw it all away and scattered it; of course, they did not eat anything.

His friend then said: "You scamp you, you are a great rascal. You are trying to make me eat meral leaves and dried cow-dung. Is it this you called me for?"

"Not at all, you fellow," he replied, "I understood it was taben and cakes that I tied up and brought. I ate some of it there. How on earth it has been changed into this, I am unable to say."

Adọ uni koṛae mẹnkeťa, Noa dọ okarem ńamleťa, oṛaǩ khongem ạguleťa, sẹ ọkọe emaťmea?

Adọ unreye mẹnkeťa, Miťṭań kuṛiye idiledińa, uniye ẹm gọťadińa. Ọṇḍẹ ma ṭhik piṭhạ taben lekageń ńẹlkeťa; ar jọm lạgiť judạgeko emadińte ona dọ ọṇḍẹgeń jọm cabakeťa, ar nią dọ oṛaǩte idia mẹnteko kol gọťadińa. Adọń mẹnkeťa, oṛaǩte dọ bań idia. Am iń ńẹlkeťme khan dọń mẹnkeťa, Nuige noa dọń emaea. Onka mẹnkate am dọń họhọaťmea, adọ ọnẹ raṛakatelań ńẹlkeť dọ, bań kan.

Adọ arhõe kulikedea, Henda ya, uni dọe ọkọe kuṛi kana?

Adọe metadea, Ẹya, ọkọe kuṛi kan cọe. Ona darha ṭhen kaḍań gaǩsao kan tahẽkan jọkhẹngeye hẹćlenteye bulạu gọťkidińa. Adọ galmarao baṛakateye metadińa, Delań, ale oṛaǩteń idimea, oṛaǩko ńẹl ạguitaleme. Ar ceť bań sẹ, uni dọ ạḍi mõ̱ńj kuṛi kanae. Ńẹltege iń họ̃ń mọńgọn utạrena. Mẹnkeťań, Nui kuṛi dọń hataoegea. Onka mẹnkateń bulạu calaolena, ar oṛaǩ duạrkoń ńẹlkeťtakoa, jọm ńũkeťań. Ar ceť bań sẹ ya, sẹn tora dọ baṛić iń bọtọrena; ẹnte bińko piṭi akana aema utạr, ar sanam lekan bin menaǩkoa; ar duṛuṕ lạgiť dọ onkogeko sọhọr gọťadińa. Adọ bọtọrte iń dọ onkore bań duṛuṕlena, ọtregeń duṛuṕena. Ar miť sẹnre dọń ńẹlkeťkoa, bogete hajar lekan kul tạruṕko burum baṛa akan. Adọ onko ńẹlte artẹťgeń bọtọrena, adọ dạṛ iń mẹnleťa. Mẹnkhan cekań bhulen cọń, hẹrge bań disạyeť kan. Ar sẹ nui kuṛi dọe pikṭhạ kante oṛaǩ khonge bae oḍokoǩ kan. Adọ ạḍi enae oḍoklena, adọ gạvićadeteń metadea, Delań, idi gọťkańme. Adọ daǩko tańadinteń ạbuk bọlọyen khan, bińge duṛuṕ lạgiťko beladińa. Adọ bọtọrte onare dọ bań duṛuṕlena. Ọtregeń duṛuṕente dahe tabenko piṭhạkoko emadińa. Arko metań kana, Ma jãwãe, nọ̃ǩọ̃e oṛaǩ duạrko ńẹlkataleben. Adọ unreń ńẹlkeťa, ceť bań sẹ, raj rapajkoaǩ họ̃ onkan asbab dọ bạnuǩtakoa, hankań ńẹlkeťa. Ar jọm baṛakate hukạkoń ńũ baṛakeťa. Adọ hijuǩ jọkhẹn noakoko ghẹ̃ṭ ocokedińa, ar kuṛiye mẹnkeťa, Delań, atra dhur iń idi gọťkama. Unre noa dọń ạgu dara akaťa.

Adọ uniye mẹnkeťa, Tọbẹ ya, Họṛ kuṛi dọe bań kana, uni dọe bọńga kuṛi kana. Họṛ dọ kul tạruṕ sẹ bińko dọ bacọbon ạsul akaťko. Onateń mẹneťa, uni dọe bọńga kuṛi kangea. Cekate bako jọmleťmea?

Adọe mẹnkeťa, Hẽ ya, hẽ ya, cekate cọń bako jọmlidiń, bańkhan dọń mucạťkoka.

Adọ uni họ̃e mẹnkeťa, Hẽ ya, sạrige uni dọe bọńga kuṛi kangea, Họṛ dọe bań kana.

Adọ ọnẹ onka, kathae, onko bọńgawaǩ taben khạjạṛi sẹ piṭhạ dọ nọtẹ ạgule khan dọ pheraoǩ kangetakoa. Adọ unre uni koṛae ạguleťte noa katha dọ disomre Họṛ họpọnko

drawing the smoke, metal parts and so on. What is mentioned here, is the form commonly used. When in use, the h u k ạ is frequently passed from one to another, if the smokers can use the same h u k ạ, each smoker drawing the smoke a few times. It should be mentioned that the h u k ạ is not an original Santal implement. They have got it from the Hindus, and it is not at all common. The Santals chew tobacco leaves mixed with lime.

8 The winnowing fan is of oblong shape, the front being straight and flat, the other sides having a raised rim, which is highest at the back. It is used for several purposes, for cleaning the grain and so on, but is also used as a loose kind of measure. It is made from bamboo and is of a fairly constant size.

9 See p. 54–5, notes 4 and 5.

10 See above, note 1.

11 See p. 106.

"Where did you get this?" the other boy asked, "did you bring it with you from home, or did somebody give it to you?"

The young man replied: "A girl took me along with her; she gave it to me. There it looked to me exactly like taben and cakes. They gave me separately to eat there and I finished that while I was there, and this they gave me to take along with me. But I thought I would not take it home, and when I saw you, I said to myself, I shall give this to him. That was my reason for calling out to you. And when we opened it, we both saw it was not what we thought."

"Look here, you scamp," the other one again asked, "which girl is she?"

"You fellow," he answered, "who knows who she is? While I was scrubbing the buffaloes at that water-pool, she came and duped me. We had been talking together, when she said to me: "Come along, I shall take you to our house. Come and see how we are living." Well, what can one do? She is an extremely beautiful girl. Looking at her I lost my senses utterly. I said to myself: "This girl I shall make mine." Having this in my mind I went along entirely lost. I saw their home and circumstances. I took food and drink with them. Well, what would you think, you fellow? When I reached there, I became awfully frightened. Snakes were lying there coiled up in large numbers, and there were all kinds of snakes, and these they pushed towards me to sit on. Out of fear I did not sit down on these, I sat down on the ground. And on one side I saw, look and behold, thousands of tigers and leopards were lying about. Seeing these I became still more frightened and thought of running away. But somehow or other I was at fault, I could not remember the way we came. Besides, the girl was occupied making cakes and did not come out of the house. When she at long last came out, I beckoned to her and said: "Come along, take me back." Then they gave me water, and having washed my hands I went into the house, and they pushed a snake towards me to sit on. Out of fear I did not sit down on that. When I had sat down on the ground, they gave me curds, taben and cakes and said to me: "Well, son-in-law, here you are, have a look at our house and our circumstances." Then I looked round, you have no idea, kings and princes have not household goods like those. So it looked to me. Having had my food, I had a smoke from a huka. When I came away, they made me tie these things up in my cloth, and the girl said to me: "Come along, I shall see you half way off." Then I brought this along with me."

His friend then said: "Well then, she cannot be a human woman[10], she must be a bonga girl. It is a wonder they did not eat you."

"Yes, yes," he replied, "it certainly is a wonder they did not eat me; then it would have been the end of me."

"Yes, surely," the other one agreed, "she is certainly a bonga girl; she is not a human girl."

In such a way, people tell, if you bring the *taben, khajari*[11], or the cakes of the bongas here, those things are changed. Since this young man brought this stuff, the story has

ṭhen pasnao akana, ar noa katha dọ sanam họrko bạḍaegea, baṅma, piṭhạ taben dọ nonka bọdọlok̓ kantakoa.

Adọ ẹnẹ inkin koṛa dọ ẹnḍẹ khonge apan ạpin oṛak̓tekin hẹć baṛayena. Ar uni koṛa dọ ạuriko bạhuae hạbić uni boṅga kuṛi sọṅgẹ dọe tahẽkana. Ar koṛatekoak̓ oṛak̓te hõe hijuk̓ kan tahẽkangea, mẹnkhan sọdọr dọ bae sọdọrlena, ar daka utu hõ bae jọmlet̓takoa. Ar cet̓ baṅ sẹ, nui kuṛiye bạhuen khan dọ, bẹbạṛićko kisạ̃ṛena, ar gại kaḍa, mẹrọm bhiḍi ạḍiko baḍhaoentakoa, ar oṛak̓ko hõ khub lạṭuentakoa, sẹ khub sẽṛã sẽṛã oṛak̓ko benao idiket̓a, adọ oṛak̓ duạrko hõ khub hamram bakhọl ạikạuentakoa. Adọ uni koṛako bạhuade khan, boṅga kuṛi dọe bạgiket̓a. Adọ ẹnẹ nia katha dọ cabayena.

Adọ ini dosra koṛa reak̓ katha nẹtẹ dọṅ lại̇et̓ kana, uni cet̓koe ceka akat̓a, onako reak̓ katha.

Adọ nui hõ kaḍa gupi koṛageye tahẽkana, adọ gupi tulućge ạḍiye banamet̓ tahẽkana. Khange Asaṛ cando jọkhẹn mit̓ din dọ baṛeg mucạt̓ bạihạṛre ạyuṕ ṅuhum jọkhẹn kaḍae ṭekao akat̓ko tahẽkana. Adọ ṅuhumen khan, kaḍa hõ ạḍiko ạtiṅ kana. Adọ cẹnḍẹṅre duṛuṕkate nui koṛa dọe banamjoṅ kana are sereṅet̓a.

Khange mit̓ṭẹn boṅga kuṛi dọ tinre cọṅ hẹćkate ato kuṛi chinte uni koṛawak̓ dea sẹćre dọ hẹćkateye teṅgo akana; ar un hạbić uni koṛa dọ bae disạyede tahẽkana.

Khangeye tẹrdẹćket̓ khan dọ, uni kuṛiak̓ umul dọ koṛa samaṅ sẹnge sẹn akantaea. Adọ cekate cọṅ ona umule ṅẹl ṭhikket̓, hoṛak̓ umul leka ṅẹlok̓ kan. Khangeye bẹṅgẹt̓ ạcur gọtket̓ khan dọ, phalna kuṛi lekae ṅẹl gọtkedea. Khangeye kulikedea, ọkọe kanam mẹnte.

Adoe mẹnket̓a, Iṅge.

Adọ aṛaṅe aṅjọm ṭhikkede khane metadea, Tinre cọṅ nọnḍẹ hẹćkatem teṅgo akan? Disạ hõ baṅ disạ hẹćletmea, ar am hõ cet̓ hõ bam rọṛ saḍeyet̓a.

Adọ uni kuṛiye mẹnket̓a, Bak̓namgem sạrdi akat̓te cet̓ hõ baṅ metam kana. Iṅ hõ onageṅ aṅjọmjoṅ kana.

Adọ koṛae mẹnket̓a, Cet̓ lagat̓em hẹć akana?

Adọ kuṛiye mẹnket̓a, Amge banamtem bulạu ạgukidiṅa. Ạḍi jutem banamet̓te bam bulạukidiṅa?

Adọ koṛae mẹnket̓a, Ma tọbẹ khan duṛuṕme.

Adọ ẹnẹye duṛuṕen khan dọ, uni sẹne gẹsrọk̓ sorente jaṅgae saṕkedetekin ṭhikket̓a. Adọ mọkọṅ baṛakate cet̓ galmarao cọkin ẹhọṕket̓, onategekin lobdhaoena, bak̓nam dọe hiṛiṅket̓a. Adọ pọhrẹk pọhrẹk sanaye pichekin kajet̓ kana. Khange bana hoṛak̓ jivi dọ tọl cabayentakina, adọ alo chapaḍao lekakin ạikạuet̓a.

---

11 Khạjạri is the Santali name for parched rice, very often used as food, when there is no time or opportunity for cooking. It is the same as is at the present day called Japanese rice in Norway. Khạjạri is mostly prepared by some Hindu castes, but some Santal women also know how to make it. See above, note 6.

12 The idea seems to be that, if a *bonga* would partake of human food, she would lose "caste", so to say, and would be shown up.

13 14 See p. 108.

been spread among the Santals in this country, and it is known to everybody, their cakes and taben are changed as told.

Those two boys now went from there to their respective homes. But the young man about whom this tale is told continued to live with that bonga girl until he was married. And the girl also was in the habit of coming to the house of the young man's parents; but she did not show herself, nor did she eat their rice and curry[12]. It is a wonder, when this girl was married, they became awfully rich, their cattle and buffaloes, their sheep and goats increased manifold; their houses also became very large, i. e., they built big, big houses, one after the other, and so their buildings and houses were felt to be like palaces, nothing wanting. When they got a wife for this young man, the bonga girl left.

Now, there this story is at an end.

Now I am going to tell the story of the other young man, the story of what he did.

This young man was also a buffalo-herd, and while herding he was in the habit of playing his fiddle[13]. One day in the month of asar[14] it so happened, that he was watching, in the evening after sunset, the buffaloes grazing near some low-lying paddy-fields at the end of the field on which the house was standing. As it became twilight, the buffaloes were eagerly grazing, and the young man was sitting on a bare spot above them, fiddling and singing.

While he was doing this, a bonga girl had come in the likeness of a village girl and was standing behind the back of the young man, and for some time he was not aware of her being there. But when the moon rose, the shadow of the girl was cast on the ground in front of the boy, and then somehow or other he saw the shape of the shadow, it was like the shadow of a human being. When he quickly looked backwards, he saw someone looking like such and such a girl and asked her, who she was.

"It is I," she replied.

As he recognized her voice, he said to her: "Since when have you come and been standing here? I was not aware of you, and you do not say a word either."

"You were so eager playing the fiddle," the girl replied; "therefore I did not speak to you. I also was listening to that."

"Why have you come?" the young man asked.

The girl replied: "You yourself have enticed me here by your fiddling. You see, you are playing so beautifully, you brought me here by that."

"Come and sit down then," the young man said.

When she had done so, the young man little by little slid over to her and caught hold of her and had his way with her. They started talking this and that and became entirely lost in each other, so that the young man quite forgot to play his fiddle. Both of them became so attached to each other that they felt it as if they could not part from one another any more.

Adọ ḍher hạbić hoeyen khan, koṛae mẹnkeťa, Ma teheń dọlań inạk hạbićkakgea. Malań apan ạpinoǩa. Ḍher ńindạyena, kaḍań idikoa. Ar am hõ pasẹć oṛaǩreko ńam baṛayetme, okayenae mẹnte.

Adọ kuṛiye mẹnkeťa, Ma tọbẹlań apan ạpinoǩa, mẹnkhan ạikạ gapa hana ṭhenlań ńapama.

Adọ koṛae mẹnkeťa, Tin ber jọkhẹn?

Kuṛiye mẹnkeťa, Tikin ṭhik jọkhẹn.

Koṛae mẹnkeťa, Acha besge, calaǩme; ạikạ alom ẹrẹńa.

Kuṛiye mẹnkeťa, Acha, ọhọń ẹrẹmea. Adọ enka cepeť baṛakate ẹnẹkin apan ạpinena.

Adọ dosar hiloǩ tikin jọkhẹn hõkin ńapamena, ạyuṗ hõkin ńapamena. Adọ onka din hiloǩ bar belakatekin ńapamena. Khange ạḍi bạṛićkin copao sạtena. Ar uni koṛa dọ bae baḍae kana, nui dọe boṅga kuṛi kana mẹnte dọ; ać dọ Họṛ kuṛigeye bade kana. Khange onka ḍher din miluạkin tahẽyena; oka dọ gupi ṭhen hõ dakae idiaea. Adọ ạḍiteťkin mel cabayena.

Khange uni dọ miťṭań jharna sọḍọǩren kuṛiye tahẽkana. Ar ona jharnare dọ akaṛ baha ạḍi bạṛić tahẽkana. Miť din dọ tikin jọkhẹnkin ńapamentekin kaj baṛakeťa. Adọ uni kuṛiye mẹnkeťa, Delań, hana jharna reaǩ akaṛ baha siť gọťańme, sunumreń bojaoa.

Adọ onka mẹnkatekin calaoena. Adọ ona sisiť jọkhẹnge cekae andha gọťkede cọń, tinre cọe aṅgen gọťkedetekin bọlọ calaoen. Adọ ọntẹ hõ nonka kuṭhạrge, nonkage bogete họṛ bạsti akane ńẹleťkoa. Adọ ḍahar ḍahartekin calaoente onko kuṛiaǩ oṛaǩteye ạyur idikedea. Adọ onkage bić gaṇḍoko beladea, adọ bọtọrte uni hõ onare dọ bae duṛuṗlena. Adọ uni kuṛiko kulikedea, Henda mãi, nui dọe ọkọe kana?

Adọe metaťkoa, Nui dọe jãwãe kana.

Adọ jaṅga daǩ ạguketťe jaṅgako ạbukkedea, ar uni jọm lagaťko tana bhanakeťa. Pạhil dọ jọl panko ẹmadea, inạkate dọ daka utu. Adọ ọnḍẹge ạḍi dinko dọhọkedea, turui cando leka.

Ar miťṭan erveltẹť koṛae tahẽkana. Adọ uniko metadea, Am dọ nui teńam sọṅgẹre tahẹnme, nui jẹmọn aloe eskaroǩ. Adọ sạri uniye tahẽyena. Ar onko kul tạruṗ dọko seta kantakoa; onkoko uni koṛa dọko tiạǩ baṛa ocoyea. Ar dinge jel tuluć dakako emaea, ar uni koṛa dọe jọm doroǩkoǩa, ceť hõ bae rọṛ baṛaea ar bae kuli baṛakoa, noa dọ cele jel kana mẹnte. Ar uni koṛa hõ ọnḍẹgeye hewayente hijuǩ hõ bae mẹn baṛaea.

---

13 The fiddle is a one-stringed instrument, much beloved by the people. Santals may sit for hours fiddling, enjoying the sound. It is, however, rather strange that a boy should take such an instrument along whilst herding cattle. They generally carry a flute.

14 Asaṛ is the first month of the rainy season in the north-eastern parts of India, from the middle of June to the middle of July.

15 A plant found in moist places, *Limnophila Roxburghiana*, G. Dox.

16 The people are constantly using oil to rub themselves in with. They prepare oil from a fairly large number of seeds. Women are, of course, making a more extensive use of oil, especially for their hair, than are the men. The perfuming here hinted at is done by soaking the stuff in the oil.

17 The same license which is allowed between a man and his elder brother's wife also exists, although not quite to such an extent, between a man and the younger sisters of his wife, provided they are unmarried. In a similar way the relationship between a man and his wife's younger brothers is of the kind called landa sạgại; their relations are of the greatest freedom and intimacy.

When they had been together until very late, the young man said: "To-day we must let it be with this. We must separate now. It is far into the night, I must take the buffaloes home. Perhaps they are also looking for you at home and wondering where you have gone to."

"Well then," the girl replied, "we must go each our way; but be sure, we must meet over there at that place to-morrow."

"At what time?" he asked.

"At noon exactly," she replied.

"All right," the young man said; "now go. Be sure you don't deceive me."

"Very well," the girl replied, "I shall not deceive you." After having arranged with one another in this way, they went each their way.

The next day they met at noon and also in the evening, and they continued to meet thus twice daily. In this way they became entirely devoted to one another. But the young man did not know that the girl was a bonga girl; he was taking her to be a human girl[1]. They remained living together in this manner for a long time; sometimes she would also bring him food where he was out herding. They became utterly attached to each other.

Now this girl was really living in a small stream with a spring, and in this stream there was an abundance of *akar*[15] flowers. One day they met as usual at noon. Then the girl said: "Come along, help me to pluck some akar flowers in that spring; I want to perfume my oil[16] with it."

Having agreed to this they went. But when he was plucking these flowers, somehow or other she cast a spell on him; some time when he was not aware of it, she spirited him off with her, and they entered the spring. There on that side it was also dry land like here, in the same way there were lots of village houses and people which he saw. They went along a road, and the girl led him along to her own home. There they put a snake before him as a stool to sit on; out of fear he did not sit down on it. Then they asked the girl: "I say, my girl, who is this one?"

"He is my husband," she answered them.

Then they brought water and washed his feet and set to work to prepare something for him to eat. First they gave him some light things, and thereupon rice and curry. They kept him there for a long time, something like six months.

There was a younger brother[17] of his wife. They told him: "You remain with your brother-in-law, in order that he may not feel lonesome." And so he did. Now tigers and leopards are the dogs of those people, and they made the young man lead these about. Every day they gave him meat-curry with his rice, and he ate; it was food, he did not say anything and did not ask them what kind of meat it was. The young man became accustomed to staying there and did not think of coming back here.

Ado khange tahẹn tahẹnte mit́ din dọ erveltẹt́ koṛae mẹnketa, Delaṅ ho sendra. Adọ sendrakin calaoena. Adọ birre jāhāegekin ńamko, heṙel sẹ ạimại, adọ uni erveltẹt́ koṛa dọe capat́ bindạṛ gọt́kotakina, ar uni kul dọkin liliạu gọt́aea, adọe gẹr gọć gọt́koa, adọ ẹnẹkin ạguket́koge. Adọ ạgukateko teke jọmkoa.

Adọ tin din hoekate cọṅ, kathae, onkage mit́ din dọ sendragekin sẹn akana, ar nui dọ kule tiạḱ oco akadea. Adọ birre sẹnkatekin ńẹlkede dọ, mit́ṭaṅ hoṛ dọ bir aṛere huruṭe kuḱṭạm kana. Ar uni erveltẹt́ koṛa dọe mẹnketa, Ma ho teheṅ dọ amge seta dọ liliạuaetalaṅme, hạni haṇḍẹ maraḱe ạtiṅ kana.

Ar uni dọe mẹnketa, Ukurić ho?

Adọ uni hurut́ kuḱṭạm horgeye uduḱ ṭhikadea, adọe metadea, Ma gọć ạguyem. Iṅ dọṅ daḱ sẹćanrege.

Khange, kathae, nui dọ ạdi garteye ror sạde gọt́ket́ khan, uni hoṛ dọe cirgal gọt́ena. Ona takre uni kul dọe aṛaḱ gọt́kadea. Adọ kathae, jẹmọnge uni kule dọn gọt́leta, tẹmọnge uni hoṛ dọ ṭaṅgateye kuṭạm daramlede. Adọ mit́ kuṭạmregeye sạt gọt́kedea. Ar uni gọć tora hoṛ dọe daṛ tap̣keta.

Adọ teṅattẹt́ bae ruạṛ kanteye paṅjakede khane ńẹlkede, kul dọe gọć ocoyen. Adọe metadea, Durhạḱ, seta dọm gọć ocọkede dọ!

Adọ uniye mẹnketa, Nui seta dọ ẹnte maraḱ tulućge bae daṛelen khan iṅ cekaea? Maraḱ ṭhengeye tobaḱ gọć ocoyena.

Adọe metadea, Bam capat́ ńọkaea? Ar uni dọe mẹnketa, Baṅ capat́adea. Adọ ọnḍẹge uni kul dọkin bạgiadea.

Ar oṛaḱre hẹćkate apat haṛam dọ lelha melha bogeteye ruhet́kedea. Mẹnket́ae, Nonkan seta nahakgeben gọć ocọkedea. Ma nui jāwāe dọ nitge idikaepe.

Adọ unre uni dọe ạgu oṭokadea. Adọ ẹnre hõ miluạ dọ bakin bạgileta. Arhõ oka oka dọ bar pẹ candoe aṅgen idiyegea. Ar nitkate uni hoṛ dọe janoḱ kana.

Adọ ẹnẹ cabayena.

---

10. Hoṛ ar toyo reaḱ katha

Sedae jọkhẹn, kathae, mit́ṭẹn hoṛ haṭiạte ḍaṅgra kiriṅe sẹnlena. Adọ joṛ sudhạge kiriṅkine mẹnleta. Ạḍi khone doṛ dam baṛayet́kogea, adọ damrege baṅ paṭaoḱ kante bae kiriṅ daṛeakin kana. Metakme unạḱ dam ma bạnuḱtae, ṭaka baṅ kulạuḱ kan. Adọ ẹnre hõe

---

18 One of the several veiled expressions for going to pay a call of nature.

19 *Jan*, a word of Sanskrit origin, means something like "the knowing one". It is used exclusively about the witch-finders. The Santals believe that formerly there were honest *jans* who got their revelations directly from the other world. Now they generally agree that they are rank humbug; still they consult them. Now-a-days they are caught and punished by the authorities. They are undoubtedly unmitigated scoundrels, responsible for much injustice and unhappiness.

10[1–3] See p. 112—114.

While he was staying there, his wife's younger brother one day said: "Come along to hunt." So they went hunting. Whoever they met in the forest, man or woman, the younger brother of his wife would knock them over by throwing something at them, whereupon they would set the tiger on, and he would bite them to death. Thereupon they would take them home and cook and eat them.

Some day afterwards, people tell, they had in this way gone out hunting, and the young man had been told to take the tiger along. When they reached the forest, they saw a man; he was grubbing roots on the edge of the forest. Then his brother-in-law said to him: "Now, to-day you must set our dog on; look over there, a peacock is feeding."

"Where?" the young man replied, "I don't see any."

The other one then pointed out to him the man who was grubbing roots and said: "Now kill and bring him. I must go at once towards water[18]."

As the young man spoke out very loudly, the man became attentive, just when he let the tiger loose. The moment the tiger sprang at him, the same moment the man met him with a stroke of the axe. With one stroke he finished him, and as soon as he had killed him, the man ran away.

As his brother-in-law did not come back, the bonga man went after him and saw that the tiger had been killed. "Dear me," he said, "you have let the dog be killed."

"Why," he replied, "this dog was unable to cope with the peacock, then what can I do? He was pecked to death by the peacock."

The other one said: "Should you not have helped him by throwing something?"

"I did not throw anything to help him," he replied. So they left the tiger there.

When they came back home, the old bonga man scolded him all round, called him a fool and so on. "Such a dog," he said, "you two have caused to be killed for nothing. Do, take this son-in-law away now this instant."

So she brought him back to this side and left him here. Still they did not leave off their intimacy. Now and then she would also spirit him away for two or three months at a time. And now this man is acting as a *jan*[19] or witch-finder.

So there this is ended.

---

10. THE STORY OF A SANTAL AND A JAḌKAL[1]

ONCE upon a time in the old days, people tell, a man had gone to a market place[2] to buy bullocks. He intended to buy a pair[3] at once. From early in the day he had been bargaining about bullocks; but as they could not reach an agreement as to the price, he was unable to buy a pair. That is to say, he had not enough for the price asked, his money was not mẹnjoṅ kana. Pasẹt́ iń ńamkatḱinge. Adọ ona bhorsate tạṅgi ńam tãrãḱ ńam ạṇḍur mạṇḍure tahẽyena.

Adọ belae ńẹle kan dọe kọcẹyen, kubelayen khangeye mẹnketa. Barea dọ ọhọń daṛelea. Acha, hẹć akan sik mitṭaṅ gan tanaḱ iń kiriń torakaegea. Arhõ jãhã hiloḱ iń hijuka, na họnẹć unreṅ kiriń idiyea.

Adọ kathae, belae jhọl phọlaoḱ kan jọkhẹn mitṭaṅ ḍaṅgrae kiriṅkedea. Ar sẹ oṛaḱ hõ sạṅgiń ńõkretaege. Khange ạguye ạguyetege ḍhere ńuhum ńindạyena. Khangeye hudis baṛaketa, ẹn kathae, Teheń dọ ọhọń tioḱ daṛelea oṛaḱ dọ, ar noa ńindạ ḍaṅgra salaḱ calaḱ dọ baṅ ṭhika, kombṛoko mẹmẹna. Jãhãge jãhã dapoṛen, teheń dọ nọtẹrege jãhãe oṛaḱreń gitić aṅgalenge. Gapa setaḱ dọń sotoḱ idiyea. Onka ać mọnre buj baṛawante mitṭẹn atoe ńamketa. Adọ ona ato sẹne ạcurena. Ar sẹye ać eskargea, sọṅgẹtenko dọ bạnuḱkotaea. Adọ atoteye rakap̣ente gitić ṭhạiye kuli baṛayetḱoa. Adọ ać eskar ma gitić ṭhạiko aṛaḱae kange, ḍaṅgra salaḱge thọ bako aṛaḱeta. Adọ onka kuli kuliteye sẹn idiḱ kana.

Adọ khange mitṭẹn tili oṛaḱe ńamketa. Adọ raca sẹnte bọlọyenteye kuliketḱoa, Henda baba ho, noakore gitić ṭhạikope aṛaḱkea?

Adọ onkoko mẹnketa, Tin họrape?

Adọe mẹnketa, Iń eskargeań ar mitṭaṅ ḍaṅgra menaetińa. Teheṅge noa hạtịa khon iń kiriń ạguyede kana.

Adọko kulikedea, Okaren kanam?

Adọe lạiatḱoa, baṅma, Iń dọ Sohodoho Jhạrịaren kanań. Adọń ńindạyente teheń dọ noakore gitić aṅgaḱ iń mẹnjoṅ kana.

Adọko metadea, Besge, dela nọtẹ hijuḱme, ḍaṅgra hõ ạgu darayetam. Ar nõḱõe noa oṛaḱre ghạnile bit́ akata, ona ghạni khuṇṭire ḍaṅgra dọ tọlkaetam, ar am dọ noa piṇḍạre gitićme, nọṇḍẹ ṭhạile aṛaḱam kana.

Adọ sạri uni ḍaṅgra dọ ghạni khuṇṭireye tọlkadetaea, ar ać dọ ona piṇḍạte rakap̣ente ọṇḍẹye duṛup̣ena. Adọ onko tili dọ tinre cọń budi baṛakette celaṅre kaṛe dọko lọhọt́kata. Adọ kedoḱko jọm baṛakate dọko jaega baṛayena. Adọ tinre nui koṛa dọ khube jạpitḱeta, unre onko tili dọ ona lọhọt́ akat kaṛete nuiye kiriń ạgu akade ḍaṅgra dọ gọṭako lasrao thopramkedea. Arko nonkaye kan, ona sud uni koṛa dọ bae bạḍaejoṅ kana.

Adọ setaḱen khan, tili dọ akoren ghạni ḍaṅgra hako pakoko raṛa ạgu gọt́kedea. Adọ onkoren ḍaṅgra dọ kaṛe jọm pạrkạu sẹ baṅ? Adọ onako thopram akade kaṛe baste nui

---

[1] In the Santali folk-tales the jackal — *Canis aureus* — plays the role in other countries generally attributed to the fox. The Indian fox is very seldom mentioned. The jackal is generally described as astute, sagacious and sharp, sometimes, but by no means always, living by his wits. He often represents the sound common-sense and justice, like in this story.

[2] A good deal of the everyday business of the people is transacted at market-places, found fairly well spread over the country. Here people bring what they may wish to sell, and here they buy the common necessaries, which they do not buy in the shops. Many shopkeepers have their own stalls at these places, the sellers mostly

sufficient. Still he was thinking by himself: "Perhaps I might find a pair." So in this hope he remained there kicking his heels and waiting, loafing about.

Then he looked up at the sun, the sun was far down, and as the time was getting late, he said to himself: "I shall not be able to buy a pair. All right, since I have come here, I must try and buy one anyhow and take it with me. Afterwards some day I may come here again, then I may buy another one."

Then just after sunset, while the rays of the sun were bright over the horizon, he bought a bullock. Now it should be noted that his home was rather far off, and as he was taking the bullock along, it became dusk and he was benighted. Then he thought and thought and said to himself: "I shall certainly not be able to reach home to-day, and to go along with a bullock now at night is not good; people may call you a thief. Be that as it may, to-day I shall pass the night in somebody or other's house hereabouts[4]. To-morrow morning I shall take him along." Having come to this conclusion in his own mind he found a village and turned aside there. Now you know, he was alone, companions he had none. Having gone up to the village he asked people there for a place to lie down in. But while they were willing to let him have a place to lie in, they would not let him have a place for the bullock also. So he went along, asking and asking for a place.

At last he reached a house belonging to a *tili*[5], and entering their court-yard he asked them: "I say, good people, might you be willing to let us have a place to lie down in here somewhere?"

"How many are you?" they asked.

"Only myself," he replied, "and I have. a bullock, that I have bought to-day at the market and am bringing along with me."

"Where do you belong to?" they asked him.

"I," he told them, "I am from Sohodoho Jharia. As I have been benighted, I intend to stay the night somewhere here until morning."

"All right," they said, "come this way, take your bullock also along with you. Look, here in this house we have fixed the oil-press[6]; tie your bullock to the oil-press pole, and you lie down in the verandah here; we are letting you have a place here."

He then tied his bullock to the oil-press pole, and he himself stepped up to the verandah and sat down there. Now those tilis had in the meantime concocted a plan and steeped some oilcake in a cooking-pot[7]. They had their evening meal and lay down to sleep; but when the young man was fast asleep, those tilis took the oilcake they had steeped in water and daubed the bullock that this man had brought with him all over with it. Of course, the young man was ignorant of their doing this.

When it became morning, the tilis quickly loosed their oil-press bullock and brought him. Now, you know, their bullock was accustomed to eat oilcake, and at the smell of the ḍaṅgra dọ curmare jal ocok̕ kana. Ona ńẹlte onko tili dọ ạḍi baṛić gulko ẹhọp̕keta. Mẹnet-ako, baṅma, Aleren ghạni ḍaṅgra dọe busạk̕entalea. Adọ inạ oḍok duạrkoren hoṛ họhọ ạguket̕koteko uduk̕at̕koa, Ma ho, ńẹletalepe, teheń dọ aleren ghạni ḍaṅgrae busạk̕entaleteye jal cikạ̃ṛede kana. Eṭak̕ hoṛren ḍaṅgra khan, nonka dọ ọhọe jallea.

Adọ uni kiriń ạgu akade hoṛ uni ḍaṅgrae laga idiyede khan, baṅgeko idi ocoae kana. Adọ onko jarwa akan atoren hoṛe bicạr ocoyet̕ko khan, onko hõko metae kana, Holare nui ḍaṅgra cedak̕ bam uduk̕at̕lea? Onate amren dọ okorle sạbud oco daṛeae kana? Adọ onka lekate onko ato hoṛ hõko bhagaokedea.

Adọe metat̕koa, Acha besge, bape idi ocoań kan khan, cet̕ iń mẹnkea? Hapẹ tọbẹ, niạ ạḍe paseren hoṛ ạgukateń bicạr gela ocokoa. Adọ judi onko hõ nonka ape lekageko bicạr-ket̕a mẹnkhan, tọbẹ nui ḍaṅgra dọ tilirengeye hoyok̕a.

Adoko metadea, Acha besge, do ạgukom.

Adọ enka mẹnkate ạḍi khọnd rọndjoń tuluće calak̕ kana. Adọ ạnạṛi hoṛ sẹ bań? Adọ ạuṛige bẹgọr hoṛte bir birteye calak̕ kana. Adọ un jọkhẹnge, kathae, mit̕ṭẹn hạpuk̕ dọe uḍạu tot̕ gọt̕ena. Adọ uni hoṛe mẹn gọt̕ket̕a, Ọhre! dataramiń ńamlede tahẽkana, daṛ gọt̕ketae.

Adọ uni hạpuk̕e mẹn gọt̕ket̕a, Cedak̕em ńam baṛayediń kana?

Adọ uni hoṛe mẹnket̕a, Mit̕ṭań bicạr ocomea mẹnte am ṭhengeń hẹć akana.

Adọ hạpuk̕e mẹnket̕a, Cet̕ bicạr?

Adọ oṛ phẹḍ jọtọe lạiadea. Khange uni hạpuk̕ dọe mẹn gọt̕ket̕a, Ho, noa bicạr dọ algagea. Do arhõ mit̕ hoṛ ńamkom, jẹmọn ińko roṛ gọṛoań.

Adọ uni hoṛe mẹnket̕a, Acha besge, ńam ạgukoań; mẹnkhan nẹṇḍẹ baṛẹ tahẽ hataṛok̕me.

Adọ uniye mẹnket̕a, Acha, tọbẹ khan nonkatege nãhãk̕ hijuk̕me.

---

sitting or squatting on the ground under small roofs which give shadow and protection against rain, or under some large tree or the like. There are a few market-places where cattle are bought and sold regularly. The markets are held on fixed days, once or twice weekly, and are visited by lots of people, who do not only come to buy or sell, but also just to meet other people, see friends and so on. They are an indispensable part of the everyday life of the villagers. Here many social matters are taken in hand. Here things are made known, proclamations and announcements are made with beating of drums.

[3] It might be noted, that the Santals and all their neighbours use bullocks or buffaloes for ploughing and carting, and never one, always a pair at the time.

[4] Except in the large bazars, inns or what corresponds to inns are not met with. It is a very common custom to let strangers sleep somewhere round the house, but not inside. Care is shown that caste is not broken and that the women are not disturbed. As a rule people will try to find somebody of their own caste or race to pass the night with.

[5] The oil presser is called *tili* by the Santals, from *tel*; this caste is of Hindu origin. Oil is pressed out of a large number of different kinds of seed.

[6] The oil-press used by the ordinary country *tili* is a contrivance fixed in the ground, of wood, with a large bowl at the top. The seed is steamed before being put in the bowl, and the oil is pressed out by a piece of wood being moved round along the inside of the bowl. The piece of wood is fastened to a pole, to which the bullock is yoked. The work is done by the bullock walking round and round, the *tili* often sitting on the pole. The Santals also press oil of seeds. They have two kinds of presses, one a more primitive one, consisting of a large

oilcake which they had smeared on the other bullock he started licking this incessantly. When they saw this, these tilis commenced to make a tremendous uproar, calling out: "Our oil-press bullock has given birth to a bullock." Thereupon they called their nearest neighbours and showed it to them: "Look, look, our oil-press bullock has given birth to a bullock to-day; he is now licking it smooth. If it were another's bullock, he would never lick him in this way."

When the man who had bought and brought the bullock tried to drive him away with him, they would not let him do so, and when he asked the village people that had come together to judge between them, they also said to him: "Why did you not show this bullock to us yesterday? As you did not, how can we prove that he is yours?" In this way these village people also went against him.

"Very well," he said to them, "if you will not let me take him away, what can I say? Wait then, I shall bring some people from the neighbourhood and get them to judge. If they also should judge as you have done, then this bullock shall belong to the tili."

"All right," they said, "do bring them."

With this purpose he went off thinking and speculating. Now you remember, he was a stranger. So he went along at random through the forest without following any way. Then a night-jar[8] all at once flew out. "What a pity," the man said, "I met a councillor, but he disappeared."

The night-jar then spoke: "Why are you looking for me?"

"I have come to you," the man said, "to ask you to judge in a certain case."

"What case?" the night-jar asked.

The man then told everything from the very beginning. "Oh," the night-jar said, "that is an easy case. Please get hold of another one, some one or other, that he may assist me."

"All right," the man answered, "I shall fetch some one; but please, you remain here in the meantime."

"Very well," the bird replied, "so just come this way."

---

stone, into which a ring and channel are cut to let the oil flow out. This stone is put at the foot of a large tree, in which a hole is cut. In this hole a large pole is put, and the pressing is done by people sitting on the pole. The other, more common press consists of two heavy pieces of wood placed one above the other on two poles, in such a way that the lower piece is fairly fixed, while the upper one is easily moved up and down on the poles, which run through holes made in the two pieces of wood, one near each end. The steamed oil-seed is put on the lower piece in a cover made for the occasion of some kind of straw, whereupon the upper piece is pressed down with the help of a rope wound round the two big pieces of wood. The lower piece has a ring cut with a small channel for the oil to run out through. The bundle with the steamed seed is placed just above this cut out ring.

7 A small earthenware pot with a wide opening, generally used for cooking most other things of food than rice.

8 The *Caprimulgus Monticolus*, a fairly common bird in the Santal country. The Santali name is onomatopoetic, from the call of the bird.

Adǫ uni hoṛ ǫṇḍẹ khone calak̓ kana. Adǫ calak̓ calak̓te mit̓tań toyoe ńam gǫt̓kedea. Adǫe mẹn gǫt̓ket̓a, Hapẹ ho, teṅgolenme.

Khange toyoe teṅgoyena, adǫe metae kana, Cedak̓em hǫhoań kana?

Adǫe metadea, Amgeń ńam baṛayet̓mea mit̓ṭẹn bicạr ocome lagat̓.

Adǫ uniye mẹnket̓a, Cet̓ lekan bicạr?

Adǫ jǫtǫ oṛ phẹḍe lạiadea. Adǫ toyoe mẹnket̓a, Ho, noa bicạr dǫ algagea, mẹnkhan mit̓ hoṛ sǫṅgeańme.

Adǫ uni hoṛe mẹnket̓a, Ho, am sǫṅgeam lagat̓ dǫ mit̓ hoṛ iń ńam akadea. Delań uni ṭhengeń idilemge.

Adǫ bana hoṛe jarwaket̓kinte ẹtǫhǫp̓ khon mucạt̓ hạbić jǫtǫ katha ar cet̓ leka phorphundikate uni hoṛren ḍaṅgrako aṭǫk akadea, onako mit̓ mit̓te sanam kathae lại cabawat̓kina. Khange unkin dǫ bana hoṛ dǫmkin ẹm gǫt̓ket̓a. Mẹn gǫt̓ket̓akin, Delabon idilińme. Khangeye ạguket̓kina. Adǫ baṛge latarko tiok̓ket̓ khan, ǫṇḍẹ dǫ thoṛa pataṛ potoṛ munḍugea. Adǫ toyoe mẹnket̓a, Do nǫṇḍẹge hǫhǫ ạgukom. Atore dǫ seta ạḍiko gẹgẹra, ǫntẹ dǫ ǫhǫlíń sẹnlena.

Adǫ uni hoṛe mẹnket̓a, Acha, nǫṇḍẹgeń hǫhǫ ạgukoa. Adǫ sẹnente sạriye hǫhǫ ạguket̓koa. Adǫ bako ńẹl ńamet̓kinteko mẹnet̓a, Okorkotam pǫ̃c? Ạuṛigem ạguyet̓bona sẹ cet̓a?

Adǫ un jǫkhẹn unkin dǫkin oḍok gǫt̓ena. Adǫe mẹn gǫt̓ket̓a, Nukintiń ińren pǫ̃c dǫ. Adǫ dhiri gaṇḍoe bel baṛa gǫt̓at̓kina. Adǫko duṛup̓ jarwayente cet̓ko cǫń emanteak̓ko galmarao kana. Un jǫkhẹn toyo dǫe kuḍbur akana ar hạpuk̓ dǫe jạpit̓ akat̓a. Khange onko atoren mõṛẽ hoṛ dǫ ạḍi garteko rǫṛ gǫt̓ket̓a, Okorkotam ho? Cet̓ lekan pǫ̃c? Unkin makin jạpit̓jǫń kan! Nukin ki kin bicạrkea? Ǫhǫkin dhẹj daṛelea.

Adǫ un jǫkhẹnge, kathae, bana hoṛge ạḍi gartekin bẹṅgẹt̓ rakap̓ gǫt̓ket̓a. Khange toyoe rǫṛ gǫt̓ket̓a, Cet̓ cet̓ cet̓kope galmaraoket̓a?

Adǫ noko hoṛko mẹn gǫt̓ket̓a, Aben dǫ eṅgate jạpit̓jǫńben arben cet̓ cedok̓ kana.

Adǫ toyoe mẹn gǫt̓ket̓a, Ẹ ho, cet̓ cǫń bań, jutgeń kukmũ gǫt̓ket̓a. Ona dǫ nonka leka kana, bańma, mit̓ṭań darhare sẹṅgẹl lagaoena ar onare ạḍi utạr hakoko lǫ gǫć akana, adǫ onkoge iń dǫ curemar iń jǫjǫm kan. Nonkań kukmũket̓a. Adǫ bhala noa dǫ cet̓ lekan kukmũ kana, ar noa reak̓ bhẹd dǫ cet̓ hoekok̓a? Dẹsẹ bhala ape mõṛẽ hoṛ lạiańtabonpe.

Adǫko mẹn gǫt̓ket̓a, Kukmũ reak̓ ṭhikạna bạnuk̓an. Oka dǫ ạuṛi hõ kukmũk̓gea. Arhõ oka dǫko mẹn gǫt̓et̓a, Dakre ki seṅgel lagaokok̓a? Noa dǫ ǫhǫge hoe daṛelena. Dak̓te ma sẹṅgẹlge iṛịjok̓ kan, cekate lǫk̓a? Noa dǫ kǫkhǫnoge ǫhǫ hoelena.

Adǫ toyo ar hạpuk̓ bana hoṛkin mẹn gǫt̓ket̓a, Acha besge. Adǫlíń kuliyet̓pea, nui peṛa hoṛak̓ dǫ cet̓pe bicạrket̓a? Lạiạlíń kanae, bańma, Hạṭ khon ḍaṅgrań kirińạgu akadea, adǫ ńindayente noa atoren phalna tili oṛak̓reń gitić kana. Adǫ setak̓en khan, ḍaṅgra dǫ bako

[9] See p. 118.

The man then went on his way. As he was walking along he met a jackal and called out to him: "Wait, please, stay a moment."

The jackal stood still and said: "Why are you calling out to me?"

"I am searching for you," the man replied, "to ask you to judge in a case."

"What kind of a case?" the jackal asked.

Then he told him everything from the very beginning, and the jackal said: "Oh, that is an easy matter; but you must get some one to be with me."

"Oh, I have got one to be with you," the man said, "come along, and I shall take you to him at once."

Having got both of them in one place he told them everything from beginning to end, all of it, what he had done, and how those people by means of tricks had kept his bullock back. Then both of them cheered him up. "Come along," they said, "take us there." The man took them with him. When they reached a little below the field on which the houses were standing — there was some scrubby jungle here —, the jackal said: "Do call them here. In the village the dogs bite; we shall certainly not go there."

"Very well," the man replied, "I shall go and call them here." So he went, called the people and brought them; but as they did not see anybody, they said: "Why, where are your arbitrators[9]? Have you brought us here to make fun of us, or how?"

At that moment those two came out, and the man said: "These two are my arbitrators," whereupon he put stones before those two to sit on. When they had all sat down together, they were talking on different subjects, this, that and the other. During this the jackal was sitting with his head bent down, and the night-jar was asleep. The village councillors then called out loudly: "Why, where are your ones? What kind of arbitrators! These two, well, they are sleeping. These two! what! should these judge? They will never be able to manage it."

At that moment both of them suddenly looked up with a start. "What, what, what?" the jackal called out, "what are you talking?"

Then those people said: "You two sleep on, then you will become what-what-what."

"I say, sirs," the jackal spoke, "whatever it was, I had a wonderful dream; it was this way: a waterpool had caught fire, and an immense number of fish had been burnt to death in that pool, and I was eating those as fast as I could. This is what I was dreaming. I wonder what kind of a dream this is, and what its meaning might be. Please, you high village council, tell me and all of us, what the meaning is."

"There is no certainty about dreams," they replied; "sometimes dreams also are utter nonsense." Again others of them said: "Have you ever heard that water catches fire? It is impossible that such things should happen. Fire is, of course, quenched by water; how should water burn? Such a thing could never happen at all."

Then the jackal and the night-jar said, both of them at the same time: "Very well. Then we ask you: what have you judged in this our friend's case? He tells us: I had idi ocoań kana. Mẹnetako, Nui dọ aleren ghạni ḍańgrageye busạk akadea. Amren dọ bale ńẹl akadea. Adọ ape atoren họṛ noa reak cetpe bicạrkettabona? Ona lạiańpe. Ar bujpe, nui dọ etạk disomren họṛ kanae. Mittẹn kaj bastẹte noṇḍẹye heclena, ar nuiren eṅga apa dọ noṇḍẹ bạnukkotaea. Onate nõkõe ạliń bir janware rak akawatlińa. Ar bujhạupe, hẹrẹl họpọn hũyạte oka bam daṛana? Kaj hoelen khan, gão goṇḍabo daṛangea. Pasẹc unre amak hõ nonka hoyoktam. Tọbẹ cetem cekaea? Adọ masẹ lạipe, cet lekape bicạrketa? Ḍańgra dọ ọkọepe ḍigriae kana?

Adọ sanam hoṛko mẹn gọtketa, Tiliren ghạni ḍańgrae busạk akadete unigeye ńamea.

Adọ toyoe mẹnketa, Besge. Adọ ghạni ḍańgrae busạk akade, onage sanam hoṛpe pạtiạu akana sẹ bań?

Adọ ạdi garte sanam hoṛko mẹn gọtketa, Pạtiạu akangeale.

Adọ toyoe mẹnketa, Besge. Ar noa ińiń mẹnlet, bańma, darha dakre sẹńgẹl lagao akante hakoko lọ gọcena. Adọ noape pạtiạuk kana sẹ bań?

Adọko mẹnketa, Bale pạtiạuk kana, ẹnte dakre sẹńgẹl dọ oho lagao daṛelena.

Khange uni hạpuk dọe ruhet gọtketa, Lelha mara hoṛ! ape leka lelha dọ duniạre hõ bạnukkoa. Kọkhọnọ ki ḍańgra busạgokpe ńẹl akawana? Gạiko busạgoka, ḍańgra dọ tisre hõ bańgeko busạgoka. Masẹ ẹnte udukańpe oka hoṛteko busạgok kana. Acha besge, delabon uni ḍańgrage udukańpe, bańma, noa hoṛteye busạk akadea. Noa dọ ạuṛiakte nui hạuṇḍikate rẹjepe mẹn akata.

Adọ bana hoṛte bogetekin ruhetketkoa. Arkin metako kana, Dini nitge ḍańgra noṇḍẹ ạgu gọtkaetaepe, ar bańkhan oka hoṛte uni ḍańgrae busạk akadea, onage udukalińpe.

Khange cap cup sanam hoṛko thir utạrena, mit katha hõ bako rọṛ daṛeata. Khange nokokin rọṛ lajaoketko khan dọ, ato hoṛte uni tilige ruhetko ruhetkedea sẹ, andha dhundko ruhetkedea. Adọ ona bạisi ṭhenge ḍańgrako ạgukadetaea, ar uni tili dọ mõṛẽ ṭaka hõko phurạnkedea. Adọ ọnẹ onkate nui hoṛak dọkin bicạrkettaea, bańkhanko atlede tahẽkana. Adọ ẹnẹ niạ katha hõń sẹsketa.

---

9 Lit. the five. A Santal village has five officials. It may possibly be due to this fact that the village council is called "the five". It is, however, more likely that the Santals have taken the thing itself as the name over from the Hindus. All ordinary village and social questions are taken before the five. The village panchayat has now-a-days very little power left, a fact which probably now everybody more or less deplores. Every one who is interested is allowed to sit in the village council; women are allowed to be present as witnesses, complainants or defendants, and may also sometimes be heard to give vent to their opinions. A person who introduces a case is permitted to bring along any outsider who may be deemed capable of looking after his interests.

10 Men only are supposed to have anything to do in the ordinary way outside their villages. Women are not thought fit to travel round on business in the country.

11 The village council has no power or opportunity to inflict other punishment than what they can effectuate on the spot. Among the Santals the party found at fault generally has to give compensation, and further to pay

bought and brought a bullock from the market. Then, as I was benighted, I passed the night in such and such a tili's house. When it became morning, they would not let me take the bullock away. They said: This one our oil-press bullock has given birth to. We have not seen your bullock. Then how did you village people judge in this our case? Tell me that. And please understand, this man is from another part of the country. He came here to do some business; his parents are not here. Therefore he has appealed to us two forest animals, as you see. Understand, being men[10] will you not now and then go travelling? When business calls, we go round to villages and hamlets. In such circumstances perhaps the same might happen to you also; then what would you do? So please tell how you passed judgement. To whom did you decree the bullock?"

Then all of them spoke out: "The tili's bullock has given birth to this one, so he will have it."

"Very well," the jackal said. "The oil-press bullock has given birth to this — you all of you believe this?"

Then all of them said in a loud voice: "That is our belief."

"Very well," the jackal again said; "now I said, water in a water pool had caught fire and the fishes were burnt to death. Do you believe this or not?"

"We do not believe it," they answered, "because water will never catch fire."

Then the night-jar started scolding: "You imbecile fools. Fools like you are not to be found anywhere in the whole inhabited world. Have you ever at any time seen a bullock give birth to anything? Cows do that, but bullocks never at all. Otherwise please show me which way they give birth to anything? Very well then, come along, show me this bullock and how he has given birth to this other bullock. It is all false, and you have intended to defraud and rob this man."

Thereupon both of them gave all of them a good scolding, and said: "Come with him, bring the bullock here now this instant; otherwise show us, which way this bullock has given birth to another."

Then they all became dumbfounded and silent; they were unable to utter a single word. When these two had made the village people ashamed by their speaking, they in their turn started scolding the tili, they scolded him something awful. Thereupon they had that bullock brought to the council; they also fined the tili five rupees[11]. In this way they judged the case of this man; otherwise they would have let him lose everything.

So now there, I have finished this story also.

---

a fine, which may be as little as five s i k ạ, i. e., five four-anna pieces, or 1¼ rupee, about 1 sh. 8d., or the double of this. It is seldom more. Both parties have to give a sum to the council, generally five or ten s i k ạ, to be spent on food or drink. Here it is a fine of five rupees, or 6 sh. 8 d.

